Table of Contents

UNIT TWO: Building Tightly Structured Paragraphs

UNIT THREE: Building Loosely Structured Paragraphs

Preface

BUILDING BLOCKS OF WRITING

Teaching writing in blocks as part of a building activity provides students with easy to remember images that help them understand and apply good writing construction. This building process helps students see how each writing block sets the foundation for the next block; as a result, their confidence in writing grows the more they learn and write. In my classes, the students learn that the first foundational block is writing correct sentences, the second is writing effective paragraphs, and the third is writing effective essays. Just as real concrete foundations require specific raw materials (sand, water, cement, and gravel) that bind and mold together into a design, each writing building block (grammar, paragraphs, and essays) requires specific ingredients. For example, in grammar, to build a correct sentence, you need nouns, verbs, prepositions, conjunctions, and so on. When writing paragraphs, the "ingredients" can include topic sentences, supporting sentences, concluding sentences, unity, and coherence.

As the second book of the *Building Better* series, *Building Better Paragraphs* builds on students' knowledge of effective sentence construction, which is covered in *Building Better Grammar*. It gets them to the next step of putting sentences together successfully for coherent paragraphs and prepares students with foundational skills for essay writing, which is covered in *Building Better Essays*.

The *Building Better* series developed out of a need to help more students succeed in learning to write effectively. Teaching writing as a building activity where concepts build on each other has worked well in my developmental writing courses. This technique of "building writing" makes the writing process a manageable one because it allows students to practice each block separately, to see how it shapes subsequent blocks, and to increase their understanding and confidence along the way. In addition, this series also developed out of necessity—a need for cost-effective books that offer simple, accurate, student-friendly explanations. Many writing books present content in too complex a manner without enough opportunities for practice, or they present so many topics that they simply overwhelm the student. The *Building Better* series evolved with developmental students in mind; however, the textbooks are designed to be flexible enough that they can also be used as quick reference guides by all college students or writing instructors. Any student who needs help writing concise and clear paragraphs can benefit from the pedagogy of *Building Better Paragraphs*. Instructors looking for a rich focus on paragraph construction, easy-to-remember, simple, and brief explanations, and a variety of practice exercises will find them in *Building Better Paragraphs*.

> "I highly commend the author for using clear, straightforward language and examples throughout the text. It is just what developing writers need. In addition, the consistent pattern from chapter to chapter will help students feel safe; they can anticipate the approach of each chapter and the sequence/kinds of activities."
>
> —Karen Taylor, Belmont Technical College

HALLMARKS OF BUILDING BETTER PARAGRAPHS

Tightly Structured and Loosely Structured Organization

Why organize patterns of paragraphs into this unique categorization of tight and loose structure? Students struggle to figure out when and how to use patterns of writing. Yet, once Gina Hogan presented the patterns in her classes, she found that students who learn the tightly structured formats (like classification, cause or effect, and comparison or contrast) first gained great confidence and proficiency in the elements a paragraph should have. Then, when they transition to loosely structured paragraphs (like narration, definition, and description), they retain their proficiency in keeping intact the basic structure of a paragraph (topic sentence, supporting sentences, and concluding sentence), yet they feel comfortable in adjusting the format and confident in their writing capabilities.

> "Most books start with the easier, more loosely structured paragraphs that students are used to writing (narration and description, also process). But because these are loosely structured, it becomes very difficult for some students to take the formal requirements of other paragraphs as seriously; some are resistant to that, wanting to go back to what they already know. But starting out with the more structured paragraphs with the initial introduction to what writing at this new level requires (when students are new to the course and at their highest motivational levels) is very smart. They are thrown into newer territory almost immediately and rely on that structure to help them instead of resisting the structure as they do when it is imposed after the fact."
>
> —Carol Pinckney, Modesto Junior College

Clarity and Consistency

Students who are being introduced to writing paragraphs need a clear, consistent approach, so they can feel comfortable with a task they believe is insurmountable. Developing writers are also usually developing readers, so all the concepts related to the writing process are carefully explained in an easy-to-remember manner.

> "It is incredibly clear. For some students, this clarity will be illuminating."
>
> —JoNelle Toriseva, Portland Community College

The chapters have a predictable flow that guides students through the writing process and through each pattern, gently reminding them of what they learned earlier as well as giving them new information to add to their writing skills arsenal. By providing students with the paragraph elements—topic sentence, supporting and development sentences, and concluding sentence—for each pattern and by showing examples, students will feel supported to write their own paragraphs. Realistic model paragraphs demonstrate the kind of writing that is expected of students.

> "I am really impressed by these chapters and feel that the clear prose, strong examples, and structured exercises offer an easy to understand and enjoyable introduction to these four means of presenting information. . . . I like the way that the text gives a definition and an example of each type of paragraph and then goes into prewriting. I also like the way the prewriting is followed in each chapter with an exercise that addresses organizing and using a topic sentence. And finally, I think the way that a group of students is asked to analyze an example before writing a particular type of paragraph is great. From the rhetorical question opening the chapters to the peer reviews at the end of each chapter, I was impressed."
>
> —Marty Brooks, John Tyler Community College

> "I like the overall organization and component parts of these chapters; the logic is compelling and they're pedagogically sound. I like the way each chapter takes you through each part of the paragraph, with a strong focus on topic sentences, all the way through the concluding sentence. The material is appropriate to the developmental level I teach. I like that each chapter ends with a list of suggested topics—a useful tool for me and my students! It's great that each chapter has a listing of transition words and phrases relevant to the particular rhetorical mode."
>
> —Steven Budd, Los Medanos College

Building Skills

Students participate in real, structured, writing exercises throughout the chapters of *Building Better Paragraphs*. The Building Skills exercises ask students to employ increased levels of effort and independence with varied opportunities to immediately practice newly learned skills, transitioning from identifying successful writing in practice sets to producing their own effective writing. Engaging, modern subjects in the Building Skills exercises serve to stimulate and encourage inventive writing from your students. Building Skills Together exercises promote collaborative work essential to writing and engagement among students.

> "First, the skills are not 'fill-in-the-blank' practice as we find in so many paragraph writing texts. They are real writing exercises. Second, the subjects for the practice are excellent; the subjects were so relevant for today's college student."
>
> —Karen Taylor, Belmont Technical College

Memory Tips and Building Tips

Memory Tips present students with inventive, class-tested methods for remembering writing conventions and processes, many times with a unique mnemonic device. By highlighting important concepts, students can remember the writing steps and feel empowered when they set out to do the task on their own. Building Tips offer guidance to students by way of short, practical, and essential writing tips to apply to their writing.

> "I really like the Memory Tips and Building Tips. It kind of slows everything down and lets students absorb the ideas that were covered."
>
> —Lori Morrow, Rose State College

Additional Resources

Instructor's Resource Manual. By Gina Hogan of Citrus Community College. Streamline and maximize the effectiveness of your course preparation using such resources as complete answer keys to Building Skills and Building Skills Together exercises, as well as Teaching Tips designed to guide instructors through teaching each chapter.

Instructor Companion Site. The *Building Better* series Instructor Companion Website includes password-protected PowerPoint slides to accompany the text, additional quizzing, and a digital version of the Instructor's Resource Manual. Instructors can register for access to this resource at login.cengage.com.

Aplia for Basic Writing Levels 1 & 2. Founded in 2000 by economist and Stanford professor Paul Romer, Aplia is dedicated to improving learning by increasing student effort and engagement. Aplia is an online, auto-graded homework solution that keeps your students engaged and prepared for class; it has been used by more than 850,000 students at over 850 institutions. Aplia's online solutions provide developmental writing students with clear, succinct, and engaging writing instruction and practice to help them build the confidence they need to master basic writing and grammar skills. Aplia for Basic Writing: Level 1 (Sentence to Paragraph) and Aplia for Basic Writing: Level 2 (Paragraph to Essay) feature ongoing, individualized practice, immediate feedback, and grades that can be automatically uploaded, so instructors can see where students are having difficulty (allowing for personalized assistance). Visit www.aplia.com/cengage for more details.

ACKNOWLEDGEMENTS

I am grateful to my parents, who instilled in me a strong love for learning and teaching. I deeply appreciate my husband and children for their enduring support and constant encouragement. I extend my ongoing gratitude to all college students, but especially developmental students, who allow me to be part of their academic journeys.

I am indebted more than I can say to Annie Todd at Cengage Learning for her belief in the *Building Better* series and their author, and I extend a huge thanks to Marita Sermolins, my Development Editor, for her expertise, dedication, and thoughtful supervision.

Much gratitude and appreciation is due the many colleagues around the country whose helpful feedback informed many parts of this book:

Kathleen Barlow, Martin University

Emily Berg, Reedley College

Marty Brooks, John Tyler Community College

Steven Budd, Los Medanos College

Stanley Coberly, West Virginia University at Parkersburg

Larnell Dunkley, Harold Washington College

Jennifer Feller, Northern Virginia Community College, Woodbridge Campus

Mary Jo Garcia, Community College of Baltimore County

Michael Kent, Riverside Community College

Dianne Krob, Rose State College

Lara Messersmith-Glavin, Portland Community College

Lori Morrow, Rose State College

Carol Pinckney, Modesto Junior College

Susan Plachta, St. Clair County Community College

Karen Taylor, Belmont Technical College

Julie Tilton, San Bernardino Valley College

JoNelle Toriseva, Portland Community College

Carmen Wong, John Tyler Community College

Finally, my acknowledgement section is not complete without this: I dedicate this book to my wonderful family–Halim, Hiam, Bill, Remy, and Christopher. Your steadfast belief in me gives me wings to fly high!

UNIT ONE: Building the Foundation

The Writing Process

CONSIDER THESE SAMPLE college writing assignments.

In a paragraph of 250 words, discuss the consequences of *malnutrition*.

For next week's paragraph, discuss the difference between *time management* and *energy management*.

After you read Chapter 3, write a paragraph in which you illustrate several important inventions of the 1990s.

For your next assignment, contrast two contemporary leaders.

Are you overwhelmed by the idea of assignments like these? You are certain to encounter the same types of assignments in your college courses, and this book will give you the simple building blocks you need to easily handle such college writing tasks. In college you are required to think and write about various concepts, so you gain academic skills and understand the world around you. Paragraph writing is an expected college assignment, so the more you practice writing paragraphs, the easier it gets.

WHY WRITE?

As a college student, you will be required to produce paragraphs, essays, or research papers. These written assignments help you on your journey of *discovery*—a discovery of yourself, your ideas and beliefs, and your world. Your writing shares your ideas with your audience, who responds to you. That written communication gives you the power to entertain, inform, or even persuade others.

The time you spend learning how to write paragraphs will benefit you; you will become a more practiced and mature writer, and you will find it easier to move on to writing essays. You will also learn to communicate clearly no matter the circumstance—in school, on the job, and in your personal life. The ultimate goals of this book are:

- To help you explore your own thoughts and feelings about writing issues and concepts.
- To help you become effective written communicators with the world around you.

THE WRITING PROCESS

Often, readers view only the completed product of a writer's work: the submitted paper. Readers rarely see what steps the writer has gone through to create a completed paragraph. In fact, a complete piece of writing does not happen all at once; instead, it goes through several building steps, each designed to create a stronger, polished paragraph. These steps altogether make up the writing process, as shown in Figure 1.1.

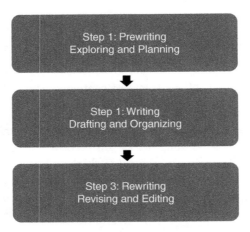

FIGURE 1.1. The Writing Process

Like any other process you use every day, such as washing the dishes, brushing your teeth, driving a car, or downloading music into your iPod, the writing process seems complicated and strange at first, but once you become familiar with the individual steps, you start doing them without thinking because they become second nature.

Most importantly, although writing generally goes through these three steps, it does not do so *chronologically*. Many times the writer may write a sentence only to change it by deleting or adding words; the writer may move a sentence to a better place in another part of the paragraph or essay; or the writer may cross out a whole paragraph or essay and start from scratch again. In other words, as a writer composes, often the three building steps of prewriting, writing, and rewriting are interconnected and overlap in that one step might happen by repeating another or while doing another. For this reason, the writing process is a **recursive** or repeating process, and it can stop, start, or go back and forth with any of the three steps. The thought of it as a series of steps makes it a manageable task. Figure 1.2 illustrates the recursive nature of the writing process where writers do not proceed in a straight line in their writing. Keep in mind, though, that writing does not have to be an overwhelming task.

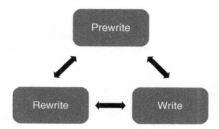

FIGURE 1.2.   The Recursive Writing Process

Writing is a skill that improves with practice. Throughout the following chapters you will become familiar with all the steps and requirements of effective writing. As you become more familiar with and master the different writing patterns, you will find yourself able to confidently evaluate and explain your thoughts about issues, ideas, and situations.

CHAPTER ONE: Prewriting and Planning Ideas

Generally, the writing process starts with a subject either generated by the writer or provided by the teacher and moves through the following steps: prewriting, writing, and rewriting.

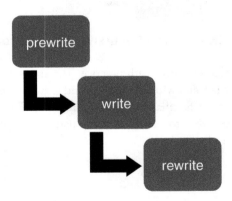

FIGURE 1.3.   Writing Process Starts with a Subject

Many academic or professional writers admit that it is challenging to get started on writing. Sometimes, you are asked to produce a paragraph about a subject of your interest. At other times, the **subject**—who or what the paragraph should be about—is assigned to you but may be intimidating because you may not know much about it, it may be boring to you, or it may be something you may not have experienced.

The writing process is generally encouraged by a sense of urgency about the subject. A paragraph is something that has to be written not just to please the writing instructor or to get a good grade, but because there is information or a point of view that you need to share with the reader. This urgency creates a relationship between you, the writer, and the reader or audience you are trying to reach and affect. Before you can reach your audience, though, you first need to understand your assignment's requirements and your purpose in sharing the information.

UNDERSTANDING YOUR ASSIGNMENT, PURPOSE, AND AUDIENCE

In college, the writing process often begins with an assignment about a specific subject. You may feel tempted to jump into writing, but it is better to think first about your assignment, your purpose, and your audience before you begin writing. In fact, these elements help inform your prewriting decisions about the subject.

Your **assignment** is the subject you are to write about and how you are required to do so. Many times an assignment given by your instructor will reveal exactly what you need to do. The first step in determining the assignment is to circle or

---

👆 MEMORY TIP

Consider the following common verbs used in paragraph prompts and what they require of the writer.

ANALYZE To separate something into parts and to discuss, examine, or interpret each part.

CLASSIFY To put something into a category with things of a similar type.

COMPARE To examine two or more things and to show their similarities.

CONTRAST To examine two or more things and to show their differences.

CRITICIZE To analyze and make reasoned judgments about something.

DEFINE To give the meaning of a term or concept.

DESCRIBE To give the physical or non-physical qualities or characteristics of something.

EVALUATE To give a reasoned opinion about something, usually in terms of the quality of a particular work, idea, or person.

ILLUSTRATE To give examples or to describe something.

INTERPRET To comment upon something or to explain its meaning.

NARRATE To tell a story.

PERSUADE To urge or influence the audience to embrace your point of view.

PROVE To argue a position by supporting your claims with factual evidence.

reflect on key words or verbs, such as *illustrate, describe, narrate, explain*. Then, once you have identified these words, make sure you understand what your instructor means by them. For example, suppose your instructor asks you to *describe* an important event in your life. This could mean you indicate and show the event and then explain its effect on your life.

Beyond understanding what is being asked of you, ask yourself these questions to focus on what the specific requirements are for your assignment:

- What subject does the assignment focus on?
- Is there a word limit, a sentence limit, or a page limit?
- When is the assignment due?
- Are you expected to work on it only at home, only in class, or both?
- Are you expected to write it on your own or with others?
- Are you allowed to revise your work?

Once you have determined the requirements for your assignment, consider the **purpose** or the reason behind your writing about this subject. Your purpose is what you hope to share or accomplish in writing this paragraph. You may want to inform, entertain, or persuade the reader. Whatever purpose you decide to adopt will determine the ideas you explore that give direction to your subject. Consider the following questions to determine your purpose:

- Should you **inform** the reader about the subject by presenting information or your feelings about the subject?
- Should you **entertain** the reader about the subject by providing humorous anecdotes, short stories, or real events about the subject?
- Should you **persuade** the reader by presenting strong evaluations or opinions about the subject?

You also need to consider who will be reading your paragraph—your **audience**. Knowing your intended audience helps you decide the extent of your explanation, your writing style, and word choice. For example, when you describe a party to your coworker or friends, the details you present and how you say them will be different with each audience. You may tell your friends more specific details than you tell your coworker. Moreover, you may use slang with your friends but formal language with your coworker. In any case, you meet the needs of the audience by changing your language and presentation. To identify your audience for a topic, develop an **audience profile** by asking the following questions:

- Who will read my paragraph? Is it just my teacher or other students in my class? How much knowledge might my teacher, classmates, or others have about my topic?

- If not my teacher or classmates, who else might be interested in my topic? What knowledge about my topic would my audience already have?
- Will my readers expect formal or informal language?
- Are the readers supportive or unsympathetic to the topic?

BUILDING SKILLS 1-1: Determining the Assignment, Purpose, and Audience

Each of the following writing prompts has a different assignment, audience, and purpose. Use the questions on assignment, audience, and purpose to think about your approach for each prompt.

1. For the other students in your class, discuss three successful study skills you have used in your college classes.
   What is the assignment? _____
   What is the purpose? _____
   Who is the audience? _____

2. For the instructor of a sociology class, evaluate the effects of fashion trends on teenagers. Be sure to revise your paragraph before you submit it.
   What is the assignment? _____
   What is the purpose? _____
   Who is the audience? _____

3. Write an e-mail to a current coworker telling her what you appreciate about her help.
   What is the assignment? _____
   What is the purpose? _____
   Who is the audience? _____

4. For the college newspaper, write a paragraph about the dangers of drunk driving.
   What is the assignment? _____
   What is the purpose? _____
   Who is the audience? _____

5. For your English instructor, write an in-class paragraph describing your funniest vacation experience.
   What is the assignment? _____
   What is the purpose? _____
   Who is the audience? _____

FOCUSING ON POINT OF VIEW

Once you determine the assignment's subject and requirements, your purpose for writing, and your intended readers, consider the perspective or point of view from which you should write the paragraph. Specifically, what pronoun or person should you use throughout the paragraph to inform, entertain, or persuade the audience.

 BUILDING TIP

You can write using any of the following points of view:

- **First-person** point of view uses the pronouns *I* or *we.*
- **Second-person** point of view uses the pronouns *you* or *your.*
- **Third-person** point of view uses the pronouns *she, he, it, they, him, her,* or names of people.

Because point of view shows the writer's relationship to the subject or from whose perspective the subject is being explained or described, it should stay consistent throughout the essay.

If you are sharing a personal story, use the first-person point of view of *I* or *we* because it is your personal story you are sharing.

> I could tell something bad would happen that day because of what I had seen and heard. I was not surprised when I heard the townspeople talk about the washed-up sailor.

If you are writing instructions or how-to paragraphs, use the second-person point of view or *you* and *your.*

> To make French fries, first you must wash the potato. Then you must peel the skin off each potato, making sure you cut out any bad spots without trimming too much. Next, you slice the potato lengthwise. After this, you fry the potato in hot oil for one minute.

MEMORY TIP

The second-person point of view is most appropriate for how-to paragraphs but is not appropriate for formal or academic paragraphs simply because it is very difficult to write from this point of view without confusing readers who might think the author is addressing them. It is best to avoid using *you* language in your paragraphs.

If you are explaining something from a detached position, use the third-person point of view or refer to your subjects by name or by pronouns such as *it*, *he*, *she*, *they*, *him*, *her*, and/or *them*. Most college paragraphs require the use of the detached third-person perspective.

> Romeo, one of Shakespeare's most memorable characters, attends a ball at the Capulet house where he meets and falls in love with Juliet. After the ball, in what is now called the "balcony scene," he sneaks into the Capulet courtyard and overhears Juliet on her balcony vowing her love to him in spite of her family's hatred of the Montagues. He makes himself known to her, and they agree to be married. With the help of Friar Laurence, who hopes to reconcile the two families through their children's union, they are secretly married the next day.

WHAT IS PREWRITING?

Determining your assignment requirements, purpose, audience, and point of view can help inform your decisions about the subject of your paragraph. Those decisions will guide your process of exploring and generating ideas. This process of exploring and generating is the prewriting step in the writing process.

When you **prewrite**, you brain storm or consider your knowledge of the subject to help produce ideas about it. Generally, this step occurs before you start writing so that you stimulate your thinking about the subject; however, you may use it any time during your writing to consider new ideas or reconsider previous ideas. Really, you think about writing *before* and *while* doing it.

In addition, prewriting helps you develop more interest about your subject. The more interested you are in your subject, the more invested and engaged you are in sharing your information and writing your paragraph. The prewriting step helps you to:

- explore your knowledge
- generate ideas about a subject
- narrow the subject to a specific topic
- plan the organizing pattern

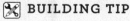 **BUILDING TIP**

If you are assigned a subject, it is helpful to put the subject at the top of the blank page before you begin prewriting. This may help you focus on the subject and may inspire a rush of ideas.

EXPLORING AND GENERATING IDEAS

The exploring and generating of ideas occurs before you start writing, and helps you discover what you may or may not know about the subject. It inspires you to consider your thoughts and feelings which, in turn, helps you to shape ideas you need for writing. Any of these methods can help you explore and generate ideas:

- free writing
- questioning or "big six" questions
- visual mapping
- reading/journaling/discussing

Use any of these techniques to investigate ideas at any time during your writing. You may use more than one technique to prewrite, or you may use some to build on others. You may begin with free writing and then take those generated ideas and map them visually in an outline form or use them for journaling. In other words, the prewriting techniques are recursive in that one can build upon another; therefore, you may use any or all the prewriting techniques for producing and developing ideas about a subject.

⚒ BUILDING TIP

Because all prewriting techniques are about exploring ideas or digging into what you may know about a subject, do not concern yourself with proper grammar or spelling as you prewrite. Your prewritten ideas need to be clear *only* to you, the potential writer, so be comfortable in expressing your prewriting ideas.

Free Writing

As its name implies, with **free writing** you write *freely* and continuously for a specific amount of time, usually five to fifteen minutes, without concern for grammar errors, spelling, or punctuation. You are recording your thoughts as they occur to you regardless of form or logic. As you free write, you may draw pictures and symbols, use numbers, or use words from another language. You might prefer typing or free typing rather than writing ideas. Whether you free write or free type, the goal is to write (or type) without stopping until your time is up or until you run out of ideas. In other words, babble on paper until you cannot anymore.

There are two types of free writing:

- **Unfocused free writing.** This is writing or typing freely about anything that comes to your mind. No specific subject or topic is assigned for an unfocused free write. Look at the example on the next page.

> The sun is out like whatever. I really don't want 2 be here right now cause
> the pencil in my hand is sticky from my dirty hands and I really liked that
> hamburger I had for lunch. Slider Burgers are the AWESOME!!! Maybe III
> have Slider's for dinner again. Wait I think my mom is making a special dinner
> to nite cause to celebrate my getting a B on my Math test. Who knew? Me
> and the letter B and Math don't go together. But hey I guess all my hours
> at the Math lab paid off FINALLY!! Oh boy boy boy that guy to my right is
> writing furiously furiously? Where did that word come from? I never use it.
> Go figure. What's he writing about? I got nothing in my head to write on and
> I don't wanna. I've always hated writing but they say I have to learn it like the
> teacher says like I can't get a job without being able to read and write. But
> seriously does writing have to be this weird like way out there weird? I think
> Im getting Math better than this writing nonesens. . .

This student's unfocused free writing exposes several ideas going through that
person's mind. For example, he or she could write about:

- Slider's Burgers
- why math is easier to deal with than writing
- overcoming his or her math anxiety

- **Focused free writing.** This is writing freely about a specific subject or topic.
  Here is an example of a focused free writing with friendship as its subject.

> ## Friendship
>
> My dog is my best friend. He is sad when I leave but is excited to see me upon
> my return. He likes to jump on me and lick my face to greet me. He is not
> a light dog. He is 78 pounds of candy-sweet love! He speaks to me all the
> time. Everyone in my family thinks I am crazy for carrying on conversations
> with him, but I am convinced he understands and responds to what I say. For
> example, when I ask him "Are you ready to go work out" he answers by barking
> loudly and running ahead of me to my work out room in the back of the house.
> He wants to have the last word like when I tell him not to beg at the table
> and to go lay down, he stares at me with his liquid golden eyes, turns around,
> plops himself on the floor and grumbles his displeasure.

This student's focused free write about friendship exposes the relationship with
his dog and their communication with each other.

BUILDING SKILLS 1-2: Focused Free Writing

Do focused free write (or free type) sessions on two of the phrases below. For each phrase you choose, spend ten minutes free writing. Remember to write or type nonstop for the whole ten minutes.

- A hero or role model in your life
- A recent event that was important to you
- Why you are in college
- A movie or book you liked or disliked

Based on your free write, what would you focus on in a paragraph if you were assigned to write about one of these topics?

Questioning ("Big Six" Questions)

Sometimes when you ask specific questions, the answers you get may trigger your mind into thinking about the subject or into thinking about it in a different way than you would have otherwise. Journalists' questions, or the "big six" questions, are used by reporters to find out more about an event or incident before they report on it. These six questions can also help you investigate your interest in a specific subject. The questions are:

- Who?
- What?
- Where?
- When?
- How?
- Why?

Consider this student's example about basketball as the subject.

Sports

Who: Michael Jordan

What: lots of money

Where: the basketball court at the school gym

When: after class

How: Air Jordan

Why: Legendary player—Best Basketball Player Ever

After answering the six questions, this student felt most comfortable with the answer to the *Who* and *Why* questions, so, in her paragraph about sports, she picked as her focused topic Michael Jordan as a legendary athlete. In other words, a combination of two of the "big six" answers allowed her to produce her focused topic.

BUILDING SKILLS 1-3: "Big Six" Questions

Use the "big six" questions (*who, what, where, when, how,* and *why*) to explore the following subjects. For each of the subjects, answer all six questions; then, identify the answer that you are most comfortable with to use as the basis for a paragraph.

- Family
- Celebration
- Websites
- Shopping

Visual Mapping: Lists, Outlines, and Cluster Maps

For many, a visual representation of ideas works better. You can "see" ideas develop creatively instead of writing long sentences. For this, you can use lists, outlines, or cluster maps.

Lists make it easy to see individual ideas as they emerge one at a time. This method works well for writers who like to organize thoughts or ideas linearly in lists. Suppose you are listing ideas about the subject of good working habits, here is what it might look like:

> Good working habits
> - Team player—works well with others
> - Cordial to other employees
> - Gives praise to others
> - Shows pride in the job
> - Punctual
> - Prompt completion of projects

Which one of the following items in the list interests you most as a writer? Isolate that one item and use it as a basis for developing a paragraph.

BUILDING SKILLS 1-4: Using Lists

For each subject, list ideas you relate to the subject. Then, for each subject, isolate one idea to use for writing a paragraph.

- YouTube
- Rap music
- Environmentalism

Outlines are extended lists of ideas that make it easier to see the flow of thoughts. They can be **informal**, with creative ways of representing ideas, or **formal**, with complete sentences and Roman numerals.

 MEMORY TIP

- **Informal outlines** are also called **topic outlines** because they show ideas developed in a few words.
- **Formal outlines** are also called **sentence outlines** because they show ideas developed in complete sentences.

Informal outlines are useful for seeing brief, general structures of the topic sentence and supporting ideas whereas formal outlines offer specific and expanded structures of how support for the topic sentences. Sometimes formal outlines may be useful later in the writing process, after you have written a rough draft, because they can help you see how the specific parts of your paragraph work together or bring order to your thoughts. The guidelines for constructing an outline are as follows:

1. Put the topic sentence at the top of the page.
2. Number the main ideas with Roman numerals (I, II, III, IV. . .), indent, and number the second-level ideas with capitalized letters followed by numbers, and so on.

TOPIC SENTENCE: _____

   I. Main idea
     A.
        1.
        2.
           a.
           b.
  II. Main idea
     B.
        1.
        2.
           a.
           b.

Informal (Topic) Outline	Formal (Sentence) Outline
Topic Sentence: Construction on college campus affects parking.	Topic Sentence: The construction of the new college campus softball field has eliminated a parking structure for 150 cars, which has resulted in several dire problems.
I. Earlier times for students	I. Students have to get to campus earlier to find parking spots.
−Arrive hours before class	A. Students sometimes have to get to campus two to three hours before classes start.
−Long walk to class	1. Students have to walk long distances from where they parked to get to class.
II. More competition for parking spots	2. They are late to class.
−Violent fights	II. There is more competition for fewer parking spots.
−Car accidents	A. There are only two parking structures available now.
III. Students park in neighborhood streets	1. Tensions rise as more students are vying for fewer parking spots.
−Block residents	2. There have been four violent attacks and three car accidents in the last semester.
−Illegal parking	III. Students park in neighborhood streets.
	A. Residents are angry.
	1. The streets are crowded with cars that block driveway access.
	2. Some cars are parked illegally, resulting in the city issuing many illegal parking tickets.
	Conclusion: The parking problems caused by the construction of the softball field require that college administrators address them if they do not want to lose students to neighboring colleges.

BUILDING SKILLS 1-5: Completing Outlines

Fill in the missing parts of the following paragraph outlines. The answers will vary, depending on your individual experiences and views.

1. Informal Outline
   Topic Sentence: A successful student has three good qualities.
   I. Good time-management skills
   II. _____
   III. _____

2. Formal Outline
   Topic Sentence: There are three main factors to making a job interview successful.
   I. The first factor is the right qualifications.
      A. A degree shows the completed education that prepares the applicant for the job.
         1. The right degree for the field adds to the applicant's appeal.
      B. _____
         1. _____
   II. The second factor is physical appearance.
      A. _____
         1. _____
      B. _____
         1. _____
   III. The third factor is appropriate behavior.
      A. _____
         1. _____
      B. _____
         1. _____

Clusters or **maps** are visual shapes like circles and lines that show how ideas are related. With both clustering and mapping, place the major idea in the middle of the page with a circle around it, "bubble" in related ideas around the main one, and connect them to the main idea. Figure 1.4 shows an example of a cluster.

You can keep branching or bubbling out from the ideas you have until you feel that you have fully explored your subject. Then, you can choose the bubbles that you are most comfortable with to elaborate on in a paragraph.

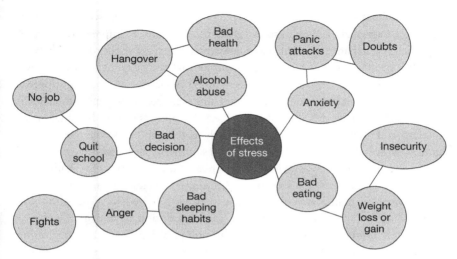

FIGURE 1.4.   Cluster Example about Effects of Stress

BUILDING SKILLS 1-6: Using Clusters

For each subject, prewrite related ideas by clustering. Then, isolate a few ideas for each subject to use for writing a paragraph.

- Internet
- Supermarkets
- Education

BUILDING SKILLS TOGETHER 1-1: Listing, Outlining, and Clustering

In a group or with a classmate, prewrite on one of the subjects listed here by using the following techniques sequentially: listing first, outlining second, and clustering third.

- Dating
- Technology
- Fashion trends
- College

Reading, Journaling, and Discussing

Sometimes, especially in advanced composition classes, a good way to start the writing process is to **read** a newspaper or magazine article, a short story, or an article off the Internet. As you read, you will take notes on the main ideas or unusual words or expressions and mark the reading with comments as they occur to you. These notes and comments will be the beginnings of your ideas about what subject on which you should write.

In some instances, **journaling** or keeping a journal is a good way to get ideas. Keeping a journal allows you to record thoughts, opinions, or impressions on paper and offers you a chance to practice writing without worrying about rules or the audience. It is good to commit to writing in your journal every day for a few minutes to jot down personal ideas, things you have learned in class or at work; controversial issues in your city, state, or country; or interesting facts from newspapers or television shows. Really, you can write about any subject that appeals to you. It is a good way to reflect and grow as a thinker and ultimately as a writer. In some classes you may be asked to keep formal journals in which you summarize and respond to something you have read. These classes require your active involvement with the reading and rely on sharing experiences and feedback with your classmates or within your writing.

For some journaling assignments, you may be required to write summaries about what you read. A **summary** is a brief description of the main events in the story. It needs to include only the chronological highlights (the beginning, middle, and end) of what happened. A summary does not express your opinion as a writer, but instead retells the key events in your own words.

Discussing is the act of talking over your ideas with friends, relatives, classmates, or teachers. Sometimes someone else will have a different way of looking at things that will help you develop more ideas. Be sure to record notes from the discussion so that you can use them later for your writing. *Note:* In literature courses or advanced English courses, you may be asked to do all three—reading, journaling, and discussing—before you are assigned a subject to write about. These classes rely on your engaging in readings and sharing your experiences and feedback.

BUILDING SKILLS 1-7: Reading, Journaling, and Discussing

As you read this excerpt, underline unusual words or make comments in the margins. Then answer the questions that follow to practice reading, journaling, and discussing.

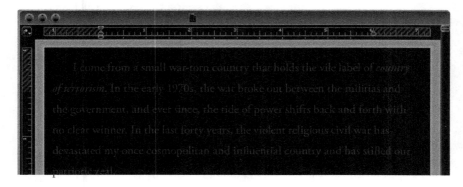

I come from a small war-torn country that holds the vile label of *country of terrorism*. In the early 1970s, the war broke out between the militias and the government, and ever since, the tide of power shifts back and forth with no clear winner. In the last forty years, the violent religious civil war has devastated my once cosmopolitan and influential country and has stifled our patriotic zeal.

I spent the early years of my childhood in this vicious environment and recognized that fanatics assassinated people including my loved ones because of their religion or political affiliation. Until the age of fourteen, my days consisted of walking cautiously in landmine-filled areas, ducking the shelling of cannons, running to underground shelters, living for days with no water or food, and listening to the whistle of rockets to hear if they were incoming or outgoing. To this day, I can still smell the noxious smoke from burning houses, the odious scent of decomposing corpses, and the putrid smell of unwashed human bodies at the bomb shelters.

Beyond all that, the pain of losing my childhood home and my loved ones never went away, and the memory of seeing my best friend blown to bits in front of my very eyes haunted me relentlessly. What did innocent thirteen-year-old Jenny ever do to anyone to deserve such a gruesome death? I did not speak for an entire year after that day. How could I when she was silenced forever? Mutely, I raged, I wailed, and I screamed at the injustice of the world, at my religion, at their religion, at my parents, at her parents, at my country but to no avail; bombs continued to descend with no rhyme or reason snuffing out our lives like candles blown out by the wind.

Years later, I realized the war and her death, more than anything, taught me to hate the injustice of ignorance, yet they encouraged me to develop resiliency in the face of adversity. Ultimately, they inspired me to take a stand against ignorance and to turn my frustrations into the meaningful vocation of Ambassador of Goodwill for the Red Cross.

1. Summarize what you have read in this excerpt.
2. Write a journal responding (negatively or positively) to this reading excerpt.
3. Share your journal entry with classmates during an in-class discussion.

> ### 👆 MEMORY TIP
> Prewriting includes the following four techniques:
> - Free writing
> - "Big six" questions
> - Visual mapping: listing, outlining, and clustering
> - Reading, journaling, and discussing

BUILDING SKILLS 1-8: Using All the Prewriting Techniques

Choose one of the subjects listed below. Then, explore it on a separate paper by following the listed sequence of prewriting techniques.

Subjects:

- Rules
- Saving money
- Popular websites
- Drivers

Subject Chosen: _____

Prewriting Techniques:

- Free write
- "Big six" questions
- Listing or clustering
- Informal or formal outline
- Reading and journaling (Find an article on the Internet or through your college's library related to your chosen subject.)

NARROWING THE SUBJECT AND PLANNING THE IDEAS

Prewriting helps you explore and generate ideas about the subject, so you can discover what you would like to build on in your writing. You use your prewriting ideas to **narrow** or **focus** the subject, so you can develop one main specific idea or **focused topic** in your paragraph.

Narrowing the subject is like taking a picture with a camera. The subject is the wide-angle lens, and the individual element you have chosen to zoom in on is your topic. Suppose you are taking a picture of a garden; then, the wide-angle shot or subject is the garden, but the narrow-angle shot or topic is the red rose in the center of the garden.

> ### 🖐 MEMORY TIP
>
> Different teachers may call a paragraph's specific topic by different terms. They may refer to it in any of the following ways:
>
> - writer's opinion
> - main point
> - main idea
> - key focus
> - argument
> - focused idea
>
> - narrowed topic
> - main lesson
> - main impression
> - dominant idea or impression
> - central idea
> - controlling idea
>
> This book uses the term **focused topic** to define a paragraph's specific focus.

To narrow a subject, first look at the sentences or words in your prewriting and circle or isolate the ones you like, or that you think might work. The next step is to group similar ideas or words together to see what fits with what and where. Then, look at the connected ideas and see what seems to be the one focus that emerges. You may not use every idea from your prewriting, or you may find that you do not have enough ideas. In any case, just by looking at your prewriting and making associations between ideas, you will have a better sense of what your focus could be and how the other ideas could work as support for it. If you find that you need more ideas, do more prewriting using the same technique as the one you used before or using one of the other prewriting techniques. Consider the example in Figure 1.5.

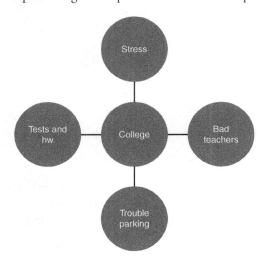

FIGURE 1.5. Narrowing the Subject of *College*

The subject or general wide-angle shot is college and the individual ideas about college or specific close-up shots may include *stress, bad teachers, trouble parking,* and *tests and homework*. Now, select one of those ideas. The bubble you choose to focus on from the cluster is the topic you will write about in relation to the subject.

Suppose you isolate stress as a *topic*. Now, to support and develop the topic of college stress, you can use some of the other ideas in the cluster such as tests and *homework, trouble parking,* and *bad teachers* for details to show the sources of stress in college. This will narrow or focus the topic further, so you can express a specific opinion about it. From your reflection on the ideas you isolate, you may produce the following focused topic: *several things produce a stressful college experience*. You could create a new cluster for stress to develop more ideas on the topic of stress in college, as in Figure 1.6.

FIGURE 1.6.   Narrowing the Subject of *Stress in College*

From Figure 1.6, you can discuss the topic of several effects of college stress. From the cluster on college, suppose you isolated *bad teachers* as your topic; now you can write a paragraph using some of the other ideas in the cluster, such as tests and homework, as details for the focused topic of *what makes for bad college teachers*. You can also create a new cluster on that specific topic to develop more ideas as in Figure 1.7.

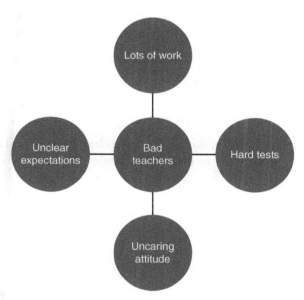

FIGURE 1.7.   Narrowing the Subject of *Bad Teachers in College*

From Figure 1.7, you can discuss several examples of things that make college teachers bad, including an uncaring attitude, unclear expectations, and hard tests.

BUILDING SKILLS 1-9: Narrowing the Subject

Refer back to Building Skills 1-8 and review your prewriting answers. Then, write a sentence that reflects a clear and narrow focus about the topic you have chosen to explore.

_____

_____

_____

BUILDING SKILLS TOGETHER 1-2: Prewriting Techniques

In a small group, work through the following prompts.

1. Use any or all techniques—free writing, "big six" questions, listing, or clustering—to prewrite on the following subject: *The Internet.*

2. Next, choose one person to write down ideas with each group member contributing at least one idea.

3. Then, discuss your prewrite about the topic and identify interesting connections among the ideas that have been written down.

4. From these ideas, narrow the subject to one clear focus. Write a few possible focused sentences about the subject; then, choose the one all group members agree on.

5. Share your prewriting and focused topic with the class.

CHAPTER TWO: Writing Stand-Alone Paragraphs

In Chapter One you learned about the prewriting step in the writing process. In this chapter you will learn about the second step in the writing process. In this step, you compose a draft of a paragraph using the topic and ideas you generated from your prewriting. Writing a paragraph helps you bring together and organize ideas into a clear structure that flows logically and makes sense.

Many writers go through multiple drafts when writing a paragraph, and the first attempt at drafting is a **rough draft** because it tends to be a basic and unpolished version. But, the rough draft helps you structure your ideas to see if they support your topic or if you need more development. The rough draft may include unclear sentences, awkward phrases, misspelled words, and extraneous ideas; however, it is something you can build on and improve.

DRAFTING A STAND-ALONE PARAGRAPH

A **paragraph** is a group of related sentences about one focused idea. Visually, a paragraph is a block of solid writing with an indented first sentence. It can vary in length depending on the writer's purpose and assignment. A paragraph can be part of a longer piece of writing such as an essay, report, or letter, or it can be a complete piece on its own. Regardless, all paragraphs include specific kinds of sentences that organize thoughts into cohesive structures: the topic sentence, the supporting sentences, the development sentences, and the concluding sentence.

Topic Sentence

The topic sentence is the sentence in the paragraph that states the **focused topic** or the writer's opinion about a specific topic. It indicates the overall *focus* of the paragraph. Although the topic sentence most frequently appears as the first sentence in the paragraph, it may also occur as the second or last sentence in the paragraph. If it directly follows the first sentence of a paragraph, it does so because the first sentence provides an introductory statement to the paragraph. If it appears at the end of a paragraph, then the paragraph presents particular details and then concludes with the focused topic.

ELEMENTS FOR BUILDING A STAND-ALONE PARAGRAPH

Topic Sentence
   Supporting Sentence
      Development Sentences
   Supporting Sentence
      Development Sentences
   Supporting Sentence
      Development Sentences
Concluding Sentence

Sample Paragraph

Rainy days bring several negative effects to my neighbor-hood. — *Topic sentence*

The first effect of rain is traffic accidents. The slippery roads create dangerous conditions for drivers, and many times, drivers lose control of their vehicles, hydroplane, and slip off the road or crash into other cars. — *Supporting sentence*

The second effect of rain is traffic jams. The wet, slippery, narrow streets in my neighborhood require drivers to pay more attention to their driving, so they have to reduce their speeds, which slows down all the other drivers and causes snarled traffic. Sometimes, drivers slow down out of curiosity to look at car accidents on the roads. — *Supporting sentence*

The worst effect of rain is flooding. My neighborhood's infrastructure cannot hold up to heavy rain. Rainwater accumulates on the low-lying ground and causes hazardous flooding, mudflows, and road closures, which affect my neighborhood's daily rhythm. — *Supporting sentence*

I dread rainy days in my town because I know they produce traffic accidents, traffic jams, and dangerous flooding. — *Concluding sentence*

> ### ✂ BUILDING TIP
>
> Topic sentences include the focused topic or the writer's specific opinion about a topic (how the writer is treating the topic or looking at it).
>
> For example, the topic of food may turn into the following focused topics:
>
> Deadly fast-food restaurants
>
> Nutritious low-fat foods to eat
>
> Best foods for diabetics

The topic sentence cannot be a **statement of fact;** it should be the writer's **statement of opinion**. A major difference exists between a fact and an opinion. A **fact** is something that can be verified or proven.

The sun rises every morning.

You can sit, wait, and watch the sunrise to verify that it does, or you can look that claim up in a science book and find it. If it can be verified or confirmed in actuality or in a credible source, it is a fact.

Seventy-three percent of college students work part-time.

Can you confirm that number from a survey in a book? Yes. Then this is a fact; it cannot be a topic sentence because you cannot explain a fact.

An **opinion** is something that requires that its writers show you why he or she feels, believes, or thinks that way because it is not based on fact, and it is not verifiable. Each one of us has his or her way of looking at things.

California is a fun place to visit.

Does everyone in the world agree with this? No. The writer may have this feeling, but someone else might think California is the worst place to visit.

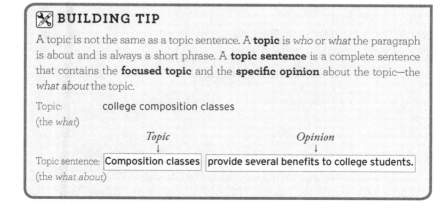

> ### ✂ BUILDING TIP
>
> A topic is not the same as a topic sentence. A **topic** is *who* or *what* the paragraph is about and is always a short phrase. A **topic sentence** is a complete sentence that contains the **focused topic** and the **specific opinion** about the topic—the *what about* the topic.
>
> Topic: college composition classes
> (the *what*)
>
> | Topic | Opinion |
> | ↓ | ↓ |
>
> Topic sentence: | Composition classes | provide several benefits to college students. |
> (the *what about*)

Since someone can disagree with this feeling, this statement is one of opinion. Now, the writer will have to share with others why California is a fun place to visit, and they may agree or disagree.

BUILDING SKILLS 2-1: Identifying Topic Sentences

The following list contains topics, topic sentences, and factual sentences. Write *T* next to the sentences that are topics, *TS* next to those that are opinion statements or topic sentences, and *FACT* next to the factual statements.

1. Poor planning ruined my grades.   _____

2. Twelve percent of death-row inmates are executed each year.   _____

3. New York   _____

4. Las Vegas is located in Nevada.   _____

5. Speeding in a car has many effects.   _____

6. Monkeys are primates.   _____

7. My father is my hero.   _____

8. Our youth get their morality from the media.   _____

9. Abraham Lincoln was born in Kentucky in 1809.   _____

10. Television ads are often misleading.   _____

11. Hollywood is in Los Angeles, California.   _____

12. Divorce can be devastating for children.   _____

13. Studying is the most boring activity one can do.   _____

14. Mark Twain wrote *Adventures of Huckleberry Finn*.   _____

15. The James Bond movies were created by Ian Fleming.   _____

BUILDING SKILLS 2-2: Recognizing Topic Sentences

Read each of the following sets of statements and then circle the one that expresses an opinion or is an effective topic sentence.

1. a) Walking to work is better than driving to work.
   b) Walkers and traffic.
   c) Walking requires no fuel.

2. a) Sources of protein in a healthy diet.
   b) Meat, poultry, and tofu are good sources of protein.
   c) A high-protein diet is a healthier alternative to most other diets.

3. a) His papers are always organized.
   b) Professor Cosgrave is an efficient teacher.
   c) He is prompt in grading tests and papers.

4. a) I bought my daughter a white kitten.
   b) Siamese cats have mellow personalities.
   c) A cat would fit with my daughter's nurturing personality.

5. a) Students enroll in college classes.
   b) Too much partying can have negative effects on college students.
   c) Students are required to take math in college.

Writing a Topic Sentence

A paragraph's topic sentence states the focused topic or opinion about the topic. In addition, the topic sentence should indicate the pattern of writing to be used for supporting the focused topic. Chapters Four through Ten elaborate on that process.

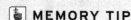

MEMORY TIP

Topic Sentence =	Focused Topic	+	Pattern of Writing
	(opinion about topic)		(illustration, cause/effect, classification comparison/ contrast, narration, description, and definition)

When you write a topic sentence, be sure to state it directly without announcing it, apologizing for it, or complaining about it. This weakens your power as a writer to influence or to inform your reader. It is important that you gain your reader's attention from the very start with your topic sentence; therefore, begin your topic sentence with strong and clear language that affirms your intentions for your paragraph. To express clear opinion statements, change the announcing, apologetic, or complaining language in your statements into a positive and pointed one.

Announcing

Incorrect:	In this paper, I will discuss the effects of smoking.
Correct:	Smoking has several negative effects.
Incorrect:	I would like to tell you about the causes of depression in seniors.
Correct:	Seniors experience depression for several reasons.

Apologizing

Incorrect: I am sorry that my position on legalizing marijuana is not what you may believe in, but I am against it.

Correct: I am against legalizing marijuana.

Complaining

Incorrect: My humble opinion on child spanking is that it is wrong.

Correct: It is wrong to spank children.

🔧 BUILDING TIP

Topic sentences never announce, apologize, or complain about your opinion. Rather, they make a clear and direct statement of your opinion. Avoid sentences that begin like the following examples:

Announcements	In this paper . . . In this paragraph . . . The subject of my paper is . . . I will begin with . . . It is my intention that I show you . . .
Apologies	I apologize that my purpose may offend some . . . Well, my humble opinion about smoking is . . .
Complaints	Although I do not like this subject, I will share my thoughts with you . . .

BUILDING SKILLS 2-3: Topic Sentences and Announcements

Read the following sentences, and write *X* next to sentences that are announcements, apologies, or complaints and *TS* next to those that are strong topic sentences.

_____ 1. The subject of this paper is how to become a good singer.

_____ 2. A real manager is confident, efficient, and encouraging.

_____ 3. Why people watch television is the subject in this paragraph.

_____ 4. Even though this is not my favorite subject, I will explain the reasons for teenage pregnancy.

_____ 5. McDonald's and Burger King share several commonalities.

_____ 6. Maria is awful to the other children and this is the issue to be discussed.

_____ 7. Some drugs are good for you but I am sorry if this subject confuses you.

_____ 8. It would seem my good friend has turned bad.

_____ 9. I will tell you the reasons for going to college.

_____10. Working mothers have it the hardest in my humble opinion.

_____11. The Latin American influence is apparent in several areas of our culture.

_____12. My uncle is a strange man, I tell you.

_____13. Learning to write effectively is a necessary skill in today's society.

_____14. You may have a different opinion about this, but I know there are several good examples of educational video games.

_____15. To begin with, a college student must overcome several obstacles to become successful.

BUILDING SKILLS 2-4: Writing Topic Sentences

Read the following detail statements for each subject. On the lines provided for you, write a strong topic sentence with a clear focused topic about each subject.

1. Subject: neighbors
   Details: loud music every weekend
            parties that go on until early morning
            unkempt yards
            leave garbage all over the sidewalk
            park their van in my driveway
   Topic Sentence: _____
   _____
   _____

2. Subject: Michelle
   Details: brings dessert when she comes for dinner
            volunteers her free time to read to cancer patients

always listens when you need advice
helps out at the senior community center
Topic Sentence: _____

_____

_____

BUILDING SKILLS 2-5: Completing Topic Sentences

Complete the following phrases to make each one a clear topic sentence. A topic and part of the focus may be given, and the missing part may be more than one word.

1. An effective manager _____

   _____.

2. Nursing is an appealing career because _____

   _____.

3. Computer skills are _____
   for today's job market.

4. Playing the lottery _____

   _____.

5. _____ is one of the
   worst things a young driver could do.

BUILDING SKILLS 2-6: Writing Effective Topic Sentences

On a separate sheet of paper, prewrite on each of the topics below; then, on the following lines, write a clear topic sentence for each topic. Remember that topic sentences must have clear focused topics.

1. Horror movies

   _____

   _____

   _____

2. Leaders

_____

_____

_____

3. Military

_____

_____

_____

4. Road rage

_____

_____

_____

5. Neighbors

_____

_____

_____

Supporting Sentences

It is your responsibility as the writer to show or explain to your reader the opinion or your focused topic. Therefore, you need to provide logical and clear support that justifies or validates your opinion about the topic. **Supporting sentences** include ideas that show, explain, or prove the opinion in your topic sentence. You decide how many supporting ideas you need to use to explain your opinion; however, three to five primary ideas (more may be used, but that is a good starting point) are commonly used as support for the topic sentence.

Supporting Sentences and Unity

In addition, supporting sentences relate directly to the topic sentence, so the paragraph has **unity** or consistency. Most importantly, uniting or linking the supporting sentences to the topic sentence increases your credibility or believ-ability as a writer. That means that, in your supporting sentences, you should concentrate on explaining the focused topic you have provided. Be sure to use supporting ideas that connect to or agree with the opinion in your topic sentence.

For example, suppose your paragraph's topic sentence is about the advantages of today's Bluetooth technology in cars.

Topic Sentence: **There are several advantages to today's Bluetooth technology in cars.**

You would need to offer unified supporting sentences that show or discuss some of these advantages. For instance, you may offer the following supporting sentences:

- **Bluetooth provides ease of cell phone use.**
- **Bluetooth technology offers consistent phone connection.**
- **Bluetooth encourages increased driver safety.**

Each of these examples helps to support the topic sentence. This means that the paragraph will have unity. However, consider this example:

Topic Sentence: **There are several advantages to today's Bluetooth technology in cars.**

- **I like several makes of cars.**
- **My friend's car mileage is better than mine.**

These supporting sentences would not produce a unified paragraph because these ideas do not relate to the focused topic of advantages of Bluetooth technology. Instead, they relate to your preferences about certain cars.

⚒ BUILDING TIP

Prewriting techniques such as listing, clustering, or outlining help you find and link appropriate supporting sentences for stronger paragraph unity.

Supporting Sentences and Coherence

Supporting sentences are also organized in a sequential manner to move the reader from one supporting idea to the next. That means sentences have to be put in a logical order, so they will be easy for readers to follow and they will provide **coherence** or clarity to your ideas. You create coherence when you arrange the supporting sentences in an order sequence of **time, importance**, or **space**. You indicate the sequence of the supporting sentences when you use **transitions**—words like *first, then, last*—to guide the reader from one idea to the next.

For example, for a topic sentence about the advantages of Bluetooth technology in cars, you could use transitions of importance for the supporting sentences.

Consider the following informal outline of a unified and coherent paragraph on the advantages of Bluetooth technology in cars:

Topic Sentence: **Bluetooth technology in cars offers drivers several advantages.**
    Supporting Sentence 1: **The <u>first</u> advantage of Bluetooth technology in cars is ease of cell phone use.**
    Supporting Sentence 2: **The <u>second</u> advantage of Bluetooth technology in cars is consistent phone connection.**
    Supporting Sentence 3: **The <u>most important</u> advantage of Bluetooth technology in cars is the safety factor for drivers.**

Lists of common transitions follow, but for a complete list of transitions, refer to Appendix B on page 000.

COMMON TRANSITIONS

Transitions showing **time** include:

after	at first	before	during	earlier
eventually	finally	later	next	now
soon	then	today	meanwhile	while

Transitions of **importance** include:

first	especially	moreover	last	
second	furthermore	principally	in fact	
most important	least of all	however	moreover	
above all	most of all	in addition	similarly	

Transitions of **space** include:

above	near	to the right	below	
at the back	on top	under	beside	
behind	on the bottom	over	between	
closer in	next to	inside	in back	
in front	to the left	on top	outside	

BUILDING SKILLS 2-7: Adding Supporting Sentences for Unity

The following topic sentences have some support. Read them carefully and add more unified support.

1. My truck is full of dirty items that need to be thrown out.
   The wadded-up Kleenex balls are strewn on the floor.
   The ashtray is full and rancid.

   _____

   _____

2. People go to the mall for several reasons.
   Some go to buy sale items.
   Some go to enjoy the bustle of crowds.

   _____

   _____

3. Depending on what activity I may be doing, I listen to three different kinds of music.
   I listen to rap while I am working out.
   I listen to classical music when I am trying to sleep.

   _____

   _____

4. The new movie theater in our area is magnificently decorated.
   Neon lights are shaped like movie reels.
   The exterior is made to look like a giant guitar.

   _____

   _____

5. Living in a small town has three advantages.
   I know all the neighbors.
   The streets are not crowded.

   _____

   _____

BUILDING SKILLS 2-8: Creating Coherence among Supporting Sentences

For each paragraph, number the following supporting sentences in order with 1 being the topic sentence. Then, state the order sequence (time, importance, or space) for each paragraph.

1.

    __1__ I had a frustrating day at work.

    _____ At noon, I discovered I had forgotten my lunch.

    _____ I got to work thirty minutes late because of traffic.

    _____ At the end of the day, I found out that I had left my briefcase at the office.

    _____ I was hungry all afternoon.

    _____ In my first morning meeting, I realized I had left my report at home.

    _____ By the time I got home, I was frustrated and tired.

Order sequence: _____

2.

    _____ Their skirts are handsomely cut.

    _____ Shoes are sensible but beautiful.

    _____ Around their necks are exquisite silk scarves.

    __1__ Fashionable women are distinguishable by their good taste in dress.

    _____ They pay meticulous attention to their hairstyles and makeup.

    _____ Their blouses and sweaters fit perfectly.

Order sequence: _____

BUILDING SKILLS 2-9: Identifying Transitions

Underline the transitions in the following paragraphs. Consult Appendix B for a complete list of transitions.

1. After Thomas and Regina married, they made several major financial decisions about their life together. For instance, they decided to live on a weekly budget to save money for buying a new house. Then, they decided on who pays which bill, so they can have equal contributions toward their expenses. Lastly, they decided not to have children right away until they have stabilized their financial situation.

2. Marlo Vine has been planning for his retirement since he was twenty-one. Last month, he finally left a thirty-year-old career as Vice President of Operations at Continental Shipping, Inc. After he retired, he wanted to stay busy, so he continued to serve as president of the Mentoring Club at his old company. Furthermore, he has held the same weekly golfing games with his three old friends who still work at Continental. Most importantly, he remains an active participant in his financial investments as he keeps track of the stock market's daily performance.

BUILDING SKILLS 2-10: Adding Transitions for Coherence

The following paragraph does not include transitions. Read the paragraph carefully. Then, consult the list of transitional words and phrases in the box below or in Appendix B and add appropriate transitions to create coherence between the paragraph's ideas.

| in the beginning | then | soon | eventually | later |
| currently | once | in no time | after | of course |

_____ Facebook is a successful social networking service that grew from one student's humble idea for connecting with friends. _____, Facebook was founded by former Harvard student Mark Zuckerberg. From his Harvard digs, he ran it as one of his hobby projects with some financial help from Eduardo Saverin. _____ Facebook's core idea spread across the dorm rooms of Harvard. _____, it extended to Stanford and Yale where, like Harvard, it was widely endorsed. _____, Mark Zuckerberg was joined by two other fellow Harvard students, Dustin Moskovitz and Chris Hughes, to help him grow the site to the next level. _____ it became a national student network phenomenon, Zuckerberg and Moskovitz dropped out of Harvard to pursue their dreams and run Facebook full-time.

Development Sentences

Your supporting sentences will be only as good as the details you use in explaining them. Once you have chosen your main supporting sentences for your paragraph, you need to provide information about each one. Your information must be in complete sentences that give clear and specific points about why and how each supporting sentence relates to the topic sentence. These specific sentences are called **development sentences.** Development sentences clarify, explain, or make it easier for readers to remember each supporting sentence in a paragraph.

You may use as many development sentences as you need to explain each supporting sentence, but consider offering different types of information such as:

- facts about the supporting sentence
- reasons for the supporting sentence
- examples of the supporting sentence
- incidents for the supporting sentence
- details to clarify the supporting sentence

👆 MEMORY TIP

An easy way to remember the types of development sentences is with an acronym known as **FRIEDs,** a term coined by Dr. Karen Russikoff.

F = **F**acts
R = **R**easons
I = **I**ncidents
E = **E**xamples
D = **D**etails
s = for plural use of facts, reasons, incidents, examples, and details

This acronym is used in this book as an optional way to refer to development sentences. Keep in mind that one sentence can have several FRIEDs in it:

Detail   *Reason and Example*

The look of the truck is masculine and rugged, and it can drive over challenging terrain because it is four-wheel drive.

Reason and Fact

See the full example of FRIEDs in the **Dream Vehicles** paragraph that follows on page 43.

As the writer, you choose the specific information to use in developing your supporting sentences. Your development sentences can include a combination of specific information, like facts, examples, and reasons. Include as many development sentences as you feel you need to explain each of your supporting sentences. The more development sentences you add, the longer your paragraph will be, but be sure the types of information you include in your development sentences are varied.

Most importantly, include relevant development sentences for each supporting sentence to add unity to your ideas. Sometimes, writers diverge or stray away from the topic they are discussing and provide sentences that do not relate to the topic sentence or to the supporting sentences of the paragraph, thus creating a disjointed paragraph. Consider the following example of a paragraph with sentences that do not support the topic sentence:

> Even though my car is twenty-years old and has more than 200,000 miles on it, I cannot manage without it nor do I want to change it. It is the only car I have ever owned. It has never given me any headaches mechanically. It's been there for me during my family separation, my party days, and my bad breakups. I record all my class lectures on my voice recorder, so I can listen to them again. I also transfer them into saved computer documents that I can access before my tests. I feel safe in it on my long reflective drives. It's seen me through so many trials and has been my dependable stress outlet. Without my car, I'd be lost.

—This is not relevant support to the focused topic of the importance of the twenty-year-old car to the writer.

BUILDING SKILLS 2-11: Writing Development Sentences

Add three development sentences (or FRIEDs) to each supporting sentence.

1. One effect of drunk driving is car accidents.
   Development sentence 1:_____

   _____

   Development sentence 2: _____

   _____

   Development sentence 3: _____

   _____

2. The most important quality in my friend is her brutal honesty.
   Development sentence 1:_____

   _____

   Development sentence 2:_____

   _____

   Development sentence 3:_____

   _____

Concluding Sentence

A concluding sentence comes at the end of a stand-alone paragraph. The concluding sentence is always the last sentence in the paragraph because it is supposed
to close off, resolve, or finish the paragraph's discussion. It does not introduce a
new idea, but instead ends the paragraph's discussion, usually by summarizing or
restating your focused topic in a fresh, thoughtful way. A concluding sentence
should leave the reader feeling that the writer has said everything needed to support and develop the topic sentence.

> **BUILDING TIP**
>
> Use concluding sentences in paragraphs that stand alone. In paragraphs
> that are part of an essay, a concluding sentence is usually not necessary.

To end a paragraph, the concluding sentence should accomplish any of the
following goals:

- **Restate** the topic sentence in different words.
- Make a final **observation** about the focused topic and/or supporting
  sentences.
- Close with a thoughtful **remark** about the focused topic.
- **Summarize** the supporting sentences of your paragraph.

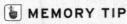 **MEMORY TIP**

Consider this acronym to easily remember the methods for concluding sentences:

RORS

for

Restating

Observing

Remarking

Summarizing

When concluding a paragraph, never announce, apologize, or complain about what you developed in your paragraph.

✂ BUILDING TIP

In your concluding sentence, <u>do not</u>:

1. Announce that you are concluding. <u>Do not</u> write, "From my paragraph, you see...", "As you can tell...", or "Now, I will close with...".

2. Add a new idea you have not mentioned previously in your paragraph that will confuse readers and leave them "hanging" or wondering why you brought up the new idea.

3. Apologize for your opinion. <u>Do not</u> write, "My humble opinion that marriage is bad for society is...".

4. Complain about the assignment or your paragraph. <u>Do not</u> write, "Even though this is not my favorite subject, I have...".

Title

You should select your paragraph's title after you have written a rough draft. The title should be:

- **Reflective of your overall discussion.** A title should come from the supporting or development sentences, never from the topic sentence.

- **Catchy, original, and short—no more than a few words**. You may use nonstandard English words so long as your language is respectful. Make your titles as catchy as possible to "hook" the readers and to compel or to excite them to read your paragraph.

  Examples of bland titles:
  > **Examples of Hobbies**
  > **The Similarities between My Two Children**

  Examples of engaging titles:
  > **My Painful Hobbies**
  > **Marriage Knot**

- **Capitalized**. Capitalize all major content words in the title. Generally, articles such as *the, a, an,* and prepositions such as *to, of, from, by, on, in, with, for* are not capitalized if they are not the first words in the title.

  > **Love in the Nick of Time**

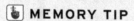 **MEMORY TIP**

In your titles, avoid using:

- Periods at the end, underlining, or quotation marks.
- The name of the assignment as the title, for example: The Examples Paragraph.

EXAMPLE OF A STAND-ALONE PARAGRAPH

Consider the following example of a well-structured paragraph.

> ### Dream Vehicles
>
> I love all kinds of vehicles, but I have three favorite ones that I would love to own. The first vehicle I would love to own is a Chevy Silverado truck. A utilitarian vehicle can carry heavy loads and withstand rough treatment. —— *Detail*
> The look of the truck is masculine and rugged, and it can —— *Detail*
> drive over challenging terrain because it is four-wheel —— *Fact*
> drive. Since I love camping, it would be an ideal vehicle to —— *Reason*

hold my camping gear and to fit all my friends. A second — *Reason*
vehicle I would like to own is the Jaguar XF. It has a unique — *Detail*
body style that is sleek, modern, yet family-friendly. It is
a four-door sedan with plush seats and a big trunk. It has — *Fact*
over 300 horsepower, yet the gas mileage it gets makes — *Fact*
— *Reason*
it a worthy commuter car. The least needed but most desired vehicle I would love to own is a Porsche Carrera 4S.
It has over 340 horsepower and weighs very little, so it — *Fact*
is one of the fastest cars ever produced. Since the first
Porsche was introduced in 1948, the German engineer- — *Fact*
ing has continued to put it at the forefront of both racing
and street cars. The Carrera body style is distinctive by its — *Detail*
curvaceous lines and low aerodynamics. It is a two-door — *Fact*
sleek bullet that can reach 175 miles per hour. It is my
dream car and the reason for my savings' account. A Chevy — *Reason*
Silverado truck, a Jaguar XF, and a Porsche Carrera 4S are
the vehicles that meet all my driving and pleasure needs.

Here are the elements in this paragraph:

- The **topic sentence** is the first sentence and the opinion part of it is the "three favorite ones I'd love to own."
- The **supporting sentences** are:
  - Supporting Sentence 1 = The first vehicle I'd like to own is a Chevy Silverado truck.
  - Supporting Sentence 2 = The second vehicle I'd like to own is the Jaguar XF.
  - Supporting Sentence 3 = The least needed but most desired vehicle I'd love to own is a Porsche Carrera S4.
- The **transition words** are: *first, second,* and *least needed but most desired.*
- The **development sentences** (or FRIEDs) for:

Supporting Sentence 1 = F = four-wheel drive
       R = Since I love camping, it would be an ideal vehicle . . . friends.
       D = utilitarian vehicle, carry heavy loads, withstand rough treatment, looks masculine, drives on challenging terrain.

Supporting Sentence 2 = F = four-door sedan, over 300 horsepower
       R = gas mileage makes it a worthy commuter car
       D = body style that is sleek, modern

Supporting Sentence 3 = F = 340 horsepower, German engineering 1948
2-door, 175 miles
R = German engineering, fastest car, dream car
D = curvaceous, low aerodynamics

Note: In this paragraph, incident and example were not used as FRIEDs; however, there were sufficient development sentences used for each supporting sentence. These development sentences make it easier for the reader to remember each supporting sentence or each example of a vehicle.

■ The **concluding sentence** is the last sentence: A Chevy Silverado truck, a Jaguar XF, and a Porsche Carrera 4S are the vehicles that meet all my driving and pleasure needs.

BUILDING SKILLS TOGETHER 2-1: Identifying the Elements of a Paragraph

Working with a partner, read this paragraph; and then answer the questions that follow.

Sloppy Bryan.doc

Sloppy Bryan

Bryan's sloppiness is a terrible habit. He is sloppy at home. He lives by himself in a one-room apartment carpeted with books, crumpled candy and fast-food wrappers, and unlaundered socks and pants. Stacks of papers cover the couch seats, and sweat-stained T-shirts bake on lampshades. The smell of week-old pizza leftovers permeates the air. Bryan is just as sloppy at work. He often arrives late, or he forgets to appear. His office desk is littered with scraps of paper and dirty coffee mugs. His files and paper boxes cover most of his office floor, and his fake plants are so dusty that a grey cloud floats down from them every time someone passes by. No one likes to go into his office, so it is a wonder he still has a job. He is the worst at his night school where his grades have suffered because few teachers will accept a student who arrives breathless twenty minutes after class has started and whose wrinkled, coffee-stained papers arrive late and spotted with dried pizza sauce or melted chocolate spots. Bryan needs to control his clopping sub-tone it controls his entire life.

1. State the subject of this paragraph.

   _____

2. State the focused topic for this paragraph.

   _____

3. Where is the topic sentence in this paragraph? Underline it in the paragraph.

4. How many supporting sentences are in this paragraph? Write them down in the order they are discussed.

   _____

   _____

   _____

   _____

5. Do the supporting sentences have a logical order to guide the reader from point to point? Circle the words or sentences that show that order.

6. Underline all the development sentences (or FRIEDs); then, choose one of the development sentences from each supporting sentence, write it down, and state the kind of FRIED it is. Are there enough development sentences to explain each supporting sentence?

   _____

   _____

   _____

   _____

7. State the concluding sentence. What method (restating, observing, remarking, summarizing) did the writer use to conclude? Does the concluding sentence close off the paragraph or does it leave the reader hanging?

_____

_____

_____

_____

8. What do you think of the title? Is it catchy? Is it reflective of the discussion?

_____

_____

BUILDING SKILLS TOGETHER 2-2: Drafting a Stand-Alone Paragraph

Working in a small group, use the prewriting you did as a group for Building Skills Together 1–1 on page 17 to plan and draft a structured paragraph about the Internet. Fill in the following format to ensure that you have all the right elements for your paragraph. Then, share your paragraph with your classmates.

1. Topic Sentence: _____

_____

2. Supporting Sentence 1: _____
   Development Sentences (or FRIEDs): _____

_____

_____

_____

3. Supporting Sentence 2: _____
   Development Sentences (or FRIEDs): _____

_____

_____

_____

4. Supporting Sentence 3: _____
   Development Sentences (or FRIEDs): _____
   _____
   _____
   _____

5. Concluding Sentence: _____

6. Title: _____

CHAPTER THREE: Rewriting Stand-Alone Paragraphs

In Chapters One and Two, you learned about the prewriting and writing steps. Now you will learn about the third and last step in the writing process: rewriting. Once you have a rough draft, you can begin the third stage of the writing process. The rewriting step helps you improve your rough draft so that your communication is logical and effective. Rewriting helps polish your paragraph, so it is free of structural and grammatical errors.

WHY REWRITE?

Rewriting is critical to good writing because the rough draft is never a perfect one. Before you rewrite, take a break from your rough draft for a while to distance yourself from your ideas and words in order to have the ability to evaluate them objectively in the rewriting process. Rewriting involves two stages: revising and editing. Revising and editing should not be done at the same time as they are considered different parts of the writing process. **Revising** is concerned with the ideas and the structure (topic sentence, supporting sentences, development sentences, and concluding sentence) of your paragraph, whereas **editing** is concerned with the grammar or structure of sentences (like verb tenses, fragments, run-ons, comma splices, punctuation, spelling, etc.). Therefore, to be a more efficient writer, do the revising before the editing so that you are cleaning up bigger writing problems before tackling the smaller ones.

Note: In some college classes, you may be asked to participate in peer feedback workshops where you exchange drafts with others to get revision and editing input. Chapters Four through Ten offer peer feedback suggestions for each pattern of writing.

Revising

Revision means to "see again." You need to "see again" your rough draft to determine if your structure, including ideas, development, and organization, is convincing and correct. During revision you are looking at the flow of your ideas. Specifically, you are looking at the elements of your paragraph: the topic sentence, the supporting sentences, the development sentences, and the concluding sentence. That means, did your ideas convey what you meant to say? In "seeing" your rough draft again, you may find that you have to change the structure, order, or content of all or some of your sentences. Read your draft aloud and mark it as you go, so you can come back and add, cut, or change certain parts. Here are some effective revision strategies:

- ☐ **Set aside your paragraph and let it cool for a while.** Take a walk, watch a show, have dinner, listen to music, or talk to friends before you try revising your newly completed rough draft. Immediately after writing, your ideas are still too fresh, and your revision effort will be ineffective.
- ☐ **Print a draft if you have typed it on a computer.** Printing a draft allows you to "see" your work laid out in front of you, so you can write comments and underline or cross out sentences or parts.
- ☐ **Review the assignment and your prewriting notes.** Before looking at your draft, reread the instructor's guidelines, your brainstorm ideas, and the model you are using for the pattern of writing.
- ☐ **Read your paragraph aloud with a "critical eye."** Consider the elements that make your paragraph clear and strong and the elements that weaken your paragraph. Closely examine the structure of the paragraph. Look to see if you have the following:
  - ☐ **Topic Sentence:** Focused topic is clearly stated in one sentence.
  - ☐ **Supporting Sentences:** Several supporting ideas are included to explain, show, or justify the topic sentence.
  - ☐ **Unity:** All supporting sentences directly relate to the topic sentence.
  - ☐ **Coherence:** Supporting sentences flow logically and smoothly through transitions (see Appendix B for more transitions).
  - ☐ **Development Sentences:** Specific information sentences or FRIEDs are used to explain the supporting sentences.
  - ☐ **Concluding Sentence:** At the end of the paragraph, a final sentence ends the discussion by restating the topic sentence, offering an observation, remarking on the topic, or summarizing supporting sentences.
  - ☐ **Point of View:** The point of view—first (*I, we*), second (*you*), or third person (*he, she, it*)—is relevant to the purpose of the paragraph and is used consistently throughout.
  - ☐ **Length:** The paragraph length follows the assignment's requirements.

☐ **Rewrite the parts that need changing.** Whatever elements are weak, write suggestions to make them stronger; you may want to consult your prewriting again to see what ideas you could add or change.

Unity in Paragraphs

It is your responsibility as the writer to show or explain your opinion to the readers. Therefore, provide logical and clear support that justifies or validates your view on the topic. The supporting sentences must relate directly to the topic sentence, so the paragraph has **unity** or consistency. Uniting or linking the supporting sentences to the topic sentence increases your credibility or believability as a writer. To that end, select and communicate supporting sentences that connect to or agree with the opinion in your topic sentence.

BUILDING SKILLS 3-1: Revising for Unity in Paragraphs

Read the following paragraphs and answer the questions that follow.

Julia Child was a famous American chef, author, and television personality. Through her many cookbooks and television programs, she introduced to the American audience French cuisine and cooking techniques. She was born in Pasadena, California. She grew up eating traditional New England cuisine cooked by the family house cleaner. As a chef, Child used ingredients like butter and cream, which caused food critics and modern-day nutritionists to criticize her cooking skills. She addressed these criticisms throughout her career and advised that focusing too much on nutrition takes the pleasure from enjoying food. Her most famous works as an author are the 1961 cookbook *Mastering the Art of French Cooking* and her television series cookbook *The French Chef.* She married Paul Child, a Boston native who was an artist and poet. Since the premiere of her television series in the 1960s, Julia Child has been the most recognized chef in the cooking industry. Julia Child's actual home kitchen was the setting for three of her television shows. It is now on display at the National Museum of American History in Washington, D.C. On August 13, 2004, Julia Child died of kidney failure at her assisted-living home in Montecito, two days before her 92nd birthday.

1. Underline the topic sentence.

2. What are the supporting sentences? List them.

   _____

   _____

   _____

3. What sentence or sentences do not relate to the topic sentence? Use the provided lines to write the sentence(s).

   _____

   _____

4. Is there a concluding sentence? What method is used (restating, observing, remarking, summarizing)? What suggestion might you make?

   _____

   _____

My grandfather Chung is a big, strong, and gentle person who took care of my sister and me when our parents died. The first thing people notice about him is his height and size. Chung is almost seven feet tall, which is unusual for an Asian man. Because of his size, my grandfather has to be careful around others. He liked to work on construction sites. When he speaks, he likes to gesture but with his big hands, every small gesture is powerful and gigantic and can hurt others if he is not careful. Whether he sits or stands, he always shifts his enormous feet for more space and comfort. His eyes are the second thing people notice about him. They are squinted and warm hazel, almost golden. They are small, somber, and filled with warmth. When he laughs, his eyes crinkle up on the sides, and his face crumbles into a funny mask. The last thing that stands out about him is his hair, which is short, spikey, and thin. Long hair is not the rage for men nowadays. My sister says it makes him look frumpy and sleepy, which means he looks unthreatening to others. Even though my grandfather Chung is large, his care of others and around others make him a gentle and comforting person.

5. Underline the topic sentence.

6. What are the supporting sentences? List them.

_____

_____

_____

7. What sentence or sentences do not relate to the topic sentence? Use the provided lines to write the sentence(s).

_____

_____

8. Is there a concluding sentence? What method is used (restating, observing, remarking, summarizing)? What suggestion might you make?

_____

_____

Coherence in Paragraphs

The supporting sentences are organized in a sequential manner to move the reader from one idea to the next. That means they have to be put in a logical order, so they will be easy for your readers to follow and will provide **coherence** or clarity to your ideas. You create coherence when you arrange the supporting sentences in an order sequence of *time, importance,* or *space.* You indicate the sequence of the supporting sentences when you use **transitions**—words like *first, then, last*—to guide the reader from one paragraph to the next. Refer to Appendix B for a complete list of transitions.

BUILDING SKILLS 3-2: Identifying Coherence in Paragraphs

Read the following paragraph and underline the transition words that show coherence.

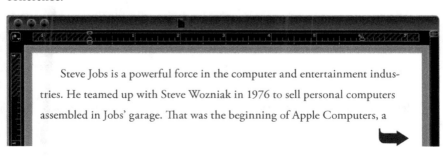

Steve Jobs is a powerful force in the computer and entertainment industries. He teamed up with Steve Wozniak in 1976 to sell personal computers assembled in Jobs' garage. That was the beginning of Apple Computers, a company that revolutionized the computing industry and made Jobs a multi-millionaire before he was 30 years old. Today, his company, Apple, leads the industry in innovation with its award-winning Macintosh computers, OS X operating system, and consumer and professional applications software. Furthermore, Apple is also leading the digital music transformation with the issue of the iPod and iTunes online store. In addition, Steve Jobs also co-founded Pixar Animation Studios. These studios have created eight lucrative and adored animated films of all time: *Toy Story, The Incredibles, A Bug's Life, Toy Story 2, Monsters, Inc., Cars, Finding Nemo*, and *Ratatouille*. Pixar has won 20 Academy Awards. Walt Disney Company purchased Pixar Studios in 2006 for $7.4 billion in stock; the deal made Jobs the largest individual shareholder of Disney stock. Steve Jobs serves on Disney's board of directors.

MEMORY TIP

Unity and coherence are two critical elements to writing paragraphs. When revising, pay close attention to your supporting sentences and transitions.

- **Unity** is about using **supporting sentences** that relate directly to the topic sentence.
- **Coherence** is about using **transitions** with the supporting sentences to move the readers logically and smoothly through the paragraph.

Refer to Chapter Two for a complete explanation on unity and coherence.

Editing

Editing means proofreading and includes making changes in the grammar of your writing. At this point you look for sentence errors in spelling, punctuation, conjunction use, pronoun use, and word choice. If some sentences cannot be easily understood when you read them aloud, edit them. When you edit, you are looking at the sentence level for how your words or sentences are used. Here are some effective editing strategies:

☐ **Read your paper aloud.** Listen carefully to your words and sentences. You can hear and see missing words, misspelled words, repetitive phrases, and incorrect constructions.

☐ **Use spell check, grammar check, and the dictionary tool.** All word-processing programs include spell check, grammar check, and dictionary options. Spell check is helpful in detecting misspelled words, but pay attention to how you've written the words because computer programs miss words like *form* and *from* or *their* and *there*. The grammar check option helps you with sentence-construction errors including verb tense, fragments, run-ons, parallel structure, apostrophe use, passive voice, and capitalization. The dictionary option helps you find the most appropriate words to use because it gives you synonyms, antonyms, and/or definitions of words. Do not assume what words mean; always look up any words you are uncertain of because using the right words makes a powerful impression on your readers. Use the thesaurus tool carefully. It provides suggestions for alternate words that mean the same thing, but do not replace a word unless you understand its meaning and know it is the right word to explain or describe your thoughts.

☐ **Examine your sentences.** Using Appendix A, study your individual sentences to see if you have correctly punctuated coordinating or subordinating conjunctions. Also, be sure that you have used a variety of sentences.

☐ **Use spelling, diction, and sentence construction questions to edit your work.**

Spelling and Diction

☐ Are appropriate and specific words used?

☐ Are slang words/phrases, text message language, or clichés used?

☐ Are words spelled correctly?

☐ Are words capitalized correctly?

Sentence Construction

☐ Are sentences punctuated correctly—no fragments, run-ons, or comma splices? (See Appendix A.)

☐ Do subjects and verbs agree?

☐ Are pronouns used correctly? Is point of view consistent?

☐ Are sentences varied in structure? (Check that not only simple sentences are used.)

☐ Are ideas coordinated or subordinated correctly?

In your paragraphs, it is important to <u>avoid</u> the following:

■ Writing in second person (using the pronoun *you* or *your*). Most academic writing requires the use of third-person point of view (using the pronouns *she, he, it, they, him, her, them*) and sometimes first-person point of view (using the pronoun *I* or *we*).

- Slang words or phrases such as *chick* (for female), *dude* or *guy* (for male), *sick* (for awesome), *my bad* (for my mistake).
- Text message language such as *LOL* (laugh out loud), *BTW* (by the way), *FYI* (for your information).
- Cliché words or phrases such as *always there for me* or *got my back.*

👆 MEMORY TIP

- **Revision** is concerned with the **idea-level** of the paragraph = topic sentence, supporting sentences, development sentences, concluding sentence, coherence, and unity.

- **Editing** is concerned with the **sentence-level** or the grammar of the paragraph = spelling, diction, and sentence construction.

Record your repeated errors, so you can see what they are and learn to avoid them or to edit for them in your paragraphs.

BUILDING SKILLS 3-3: Editing

Read the following paragraphs and underline the errors you find. Correctly rewrite the paragraph on the lines provided.

1. While its may intimidate many public speaking is a powerful skill to learn. Public speaking is the process of speaking to a group of people in a ordered purposeful manner to inform influence or entertain the listeners. In public speaking, as in any form of communication there is five basic elements, often expressed as *who* is saying *what* to *whom* using what *medium* with what *effects.* The purpose of public speaking can range from simply conveying informatio to encouraging people to act to simply telling a story. Good orators should be able to change the emotions of their listeners, not just inform them and their in lies the power to change things in our world. Preparation is one of the most important factors in determining comunication successses. One can begin by doing a detailed reserch on the topic to plan the data and focus on the intersts of the audience. People do not like presentations that go on forever. One should try to make it short and emphasizing the key points. Time the presentation such that you finish before the stipulated time and use visuals like slid shows because they effect the memory of human beigs. Laslty, practicing the speech is the best way to increse the skil in speaking to the public.

_____

_____

_____

_____

_____

_____

_____

2.   Driving back and forth to his new job created several problem for William.
He had to get up at five am to arrive at his work on time. Because he left
home so early William could know longer eat breakfast with his family
they were steal asleep when he began his work. William was often delayed
bye traffic accidents or freeway closares. Once he got to work, he was so
tired from traffic and waking up so early that he rushed his tasks and others
around him. That created bad relationships with his co-workers and created
so much stress at work for William. At the end of the day he had to make
the long drive back home and was fysically and mentaly exhausted bye the
thyme he made it around dinner time that he would snap at his children and
wife which created even more stress for him. He voweled that next time he
excepted a job it will be close to his home.

_____

_____

_____

_____

_____

_____

_____

_____

_____

_____

_____

_____

Preparing Your Final Paragraph for Submission

When you have revised and edited your paragraph, it is time to produce a clean
copy, which means you have to rewrite certain parts of your paragraph to make
all the necessary changes and adjustments you discovered during the revision and
editing stages. Follow the submission guidelines provided by your instructor, but
consider this generic checklist for manuscript submission listed in the Modern
Language Association (MLA) guidelines:

- Use only 8.5-by-11-inch paper (not torn out of a spiral-bound notebook).
- Print on one side of the paper only.

- Double-space your paragraph and do not add extra space above or below the title of the paragraph. Use Times New Roman font with a 12-point font size.
- Leave one-inch margins all around from the edge of the paper. Left align the text.
- Center the title at the top of the page. Do not underline, italicize, or put quotation marks around the title.
- Put your name, your instructor's name, course title, and date on separate lines against the left margin of the first page of your paper.
- Indent the first line of the paragraph one-half inch or five spaces from the left (hit the *tab* button once).
- Leave one space after each period and one space after each comma.
- Put the page number preceded by your last name in the upper-right corner as the header of each page one-half inch below the top edge. Use Arabic numerals (1, 2, 3 . . .).
- Make a copy of your paper or save it on a storage memory device before you submit it, in case of loss.
- Staple together the peer revision worksheets, your rough drafts, and your final draft, if your instructor requires you do so.

🔧 BUILDING TIP

MLA requirements may change, so be sure to reference the most recent MLA guidelines by visiting www.mla.org.

🕯 BUILDING SKILLS TOGETHER 3-1: Rewriting Feedback

Work with a partner or small group on the paragraph you wrote for Building Skills Together 2-2 on page 47. Revise and edit the paragraph by answering the following questions.

Revising: Idea-level

1. What is the topic sentence in this paragraph? Underline it in the paragraph and state the focused topic. Is it effective? What changes might be needed?

2. What supporting sentences are used to strongly explain, show, or justify the topic sentence? State them in the order they were presented. What changes might be needed?

3. For each supporting sentence, how many and what kind of development sentences or FRIEDs are used? What changes might be needed?

4. Is the paragraph unified? Do all supporting ideas and sentences directly relate to the topic sentence?

5. Is the paragraph coherent? Circle any transitions in the paragraph. State the order (time, space, importance) they follow. Do the transitions help the supporting sentences flow logically and smoothly? What changes might be needed?

6. Is there a concluding sentence? State it. What method (restating, observing, remarking, or summarizing) for ending the discussion is used in the concluding sentence? What changes might be needed?

7. What point of view (first, second, or third person) is used in the paragraph? Is it relevant to the writer's purpose? Is it consistent throughout the paragraph? What changes might be needed?

8. Length of the paragraph: Does the length adhere to the requirements of the assignment or to the expected length of 10 to 15 sentences? What changes might be needed?

9. Is the title catchy and relevant? What changes might be needed?

Editing: Sentence-Level
Spelling and Diction

1. Are appropriate and specific words used?

2. Are slang words, text message language, or clichés used?

3. Are words spelled correctly?

4. Are words capitalized correctly?

Sentence Construction

1. Are sentences punctuated correctly—no fragments, run-ons, or comma splices? (See Appendix A.)

2. Do subjects and verbs agree?

3. Are pronouns used correctly? Is point of view consistent?

4. Are sentences varied in structure?

5. Are ideas coordinated or subordinated correctly?

⬤ BUILDING SKILLS TOGETHER 3-2: The Three Stages of Writing

Work with a partner on using the three stages of writing. Write a coherent and concise paragraph and be sure to turn in to your instructor your prewriting activity, your rough draft(s), and your final revised draft. Use the revision questions shown in Building Skills Together 3-1. Choose one of the following topics for your paragraph:

- A favorite place
- Someone you admire
- The difficulty of living with a roommate or family member
- Athletes who are role models

UNIT TWO: Building Tightly Structured Paragraphs

NOW THAT YOU have learned about the writing process, you are ready to write paragraphs. Paragraph writing for English classes requires that you know and use various writing patterns. Some writing patterns or paragraphs follow a prescribed and formal structure, especially when it comes to the topic sentence, the supporting and development sentences, and the concluding sentence. The patterns of writing that lend themselves to strict structures are:

- Illustration
- Cause and Effect
- Classification
- Comparison/Contrast

CHAPTER FOUR: Illustration
Building Paragraphs with Examples

What do you mean when you tell a friend that a movie is good or that a restaurant is bad? Or that some new proposed laws do not seem helpful to society? To explain such statements, you would need to **illustrate** or give **examples** to clarify what you mean. Some college assignments may require that you illustrate your opinion on certain subjects.

Illustration is the use of several specific examples to illustrate or explain, clarify, or show the main point or topic sentence. Giving examples is an effective way of explaining or showing complex and abstract concepts to make them easier to understand. For example, if you are trying to show the things that distract you in a classroom, you might cite the fact that your cell phone vibrates every ten minutes alerting you about a new text message, the cute student next to you keeps sending you secret notes, or the teacher's lisp interferes with your understanding of what he says. In short, illustration gives specific and understandable examples to show the point.

WRITING AN ILLUSTRATION PARAGRAPH
Well-chosen examples are essential to illustration, and you can draw examples from personal experience, observations, or readings. Begin your writing with some prewriting activities that help you reflect on examples for your subject. As you are prewriting, make sure that your examples are:

- specific
- clearly and directly related to the subject
- interesting and believable for the reader

As a topic, consider things you would do if you became an instant millionaire. In your prewriting, you may start listing what you would do. Listing is a useful approach for illustration. Consider this example of listing:

- Party for a week
- Pay off all credit card and college debts
- Dine at expensive restaurants
- Pay for my grandfather's health care costs
- Hire a full-time nurse to care for my sick grandfather
- Pay off Mom's debts
- Buy a big house
- Buy parents their dream house
- Buy fancy clothes, jewelry, and cars for myself
- Invest in the stock market and in real estate
- Donate to cancer research and charities
- Start a company that employs others

All these examples are directly related to the topic of becoming an instant millionaire because they are about initial behaviors one might go through after acquiring a huge sum of money. They are also specific and believable because they are, in fact, things that many people try to accomplish if they had money. You could consider narrowing your prewriting to things you would do that would change your life for the better such as buying a car or a house. Or, you could narrow your prewriting from this listing to things you would do to help others. Consider that you choose things you would do to help others. Now, look at the list again and draw out the things that would help show or support your focus about things you would do to help others. Pick three specific, directly related, and interesting examples that you could use in writing an illustration paragraph about things you would do for others if you became an instant millionaire. Now that you have your examples, you are ready to begin writing your rough draft.

GENERIC PLAN FOR AN ILLUSTRATION PARAGRAPH

Topic Sentence: Focused Topic + Examples
    Supporting Sentence 1—First Example
        Development Sentences (or FRIEDs)
    Supporting Sentence 2—Second Example
        Development Sentences (or FRIEDs)
    Supporting Sentence 3—Third Example (Most important example)
        Development Sentences (or FRIEDs)
Concluding Sentence

BUILDING SKILLS 4-1: Finding Related Examples

In each list, circle the examples that fit each topic sentence.

1. Topic sentence: Exercising can be done in various ways.
     playing basketball
     the dangers of obesity
     riding a bike
     calories and fat
     walking in the park
     running on the beach

2. Topic sentence: Siblings create several disadvantages.
     forced to share
     no privacy
     companionship
     family warmth
     competition
     good support system

Topic Sentence

In illustration, the topic sentence starts your paragraph, states your focused topic or your opinion about the topic, and indicates the writing pattern of illustration or examples. Since you will provide several specific, well-chosen supporting examples to explain your topic sentence, remember to phrase the topic sentence in your own style of writing so it indicates to the reader your focused topic and your pattern of writing of illustration. In short, invite the readers to ask the question *what kind* or *which ones* when they read your topic sentence. Your supporting sentences show the reader exactly *what kind* or *which ones* you mean.

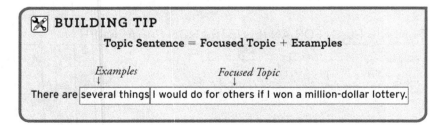

BUILDING SKILLS 4-2: Recognizing Effective Illustration Topic Sentences

Read each statement and write *TS* next to the ones that are effective illustration topic sentences and *X* next to those that are not.

_____ 1. The new art museum is good.

_____ 2. There are several issues facing our country.

_____ 3. How to unclutter your home.

_____ 4. Money is one of my obstacles in life.

_____ 5. There are several ways to join a fitness club.

_____ 6. Three techniques can help with success in college.

_____ 7. A worker at a gas station must know four safety rules.

_____ 8. Staring is an annoying habit.

_____ 9. There are three places I avoid at my grandmother's house.

_____ 10. The three most undesirable jobs are trash collecting, plumbing, and restroom cleaning.

Supporting Sentences

The supporting sentences in an illustration paragraph are the examples you use to show and explain your focused topic. How many examples you need depends on your topic sentence, but generally, three to five specific, related supporting examples are used. In the previous example on becoming an instant million-aire, the supporting sentences would be the three examples chosen from the list of examples. Consider that the following three examples were chosen for the focused topic of helping others: paying for grandfather's healthcare, helping cancer patients, and buying a house for the parents.

In illustration, examples are discussed or organized in a logical order, from least to most or most to least important or from general to specific, so you need to choose the order of your examples before you begin writing. For the instant millionaire topic, the three examples could be in whatever order you choose, but for the purposes of demonstration, here is one way to order the examples: first, the grandfather's healthcare; second, the parents' dream house; and most impor-tant, cancer patients. Now you are ready to start your paragraph's rough draft.

BUILDING SKILLS 4-3: Finding Specific Examples

Add specific examples to explain each topic sentence.

1. Of all eating establishments, cafeteria food can be the most unpleasant.
   Examples: _____

   _____

   _____

   _____

   _____

   _____

   _____

2. When they drive their cars, people can be distracted by many activities.
   Examples: _____

   _____

   _____

   _____

   _____

TRANSITIONS USED IN ILLUSTRATION

As you move your reader through your paragraph from one major example to another, use the following transition words:

also	for one thing	finally	furthermore
another	for instance	first	moreover
one example	for example	second	in addition
another example	in addition	third	specifically
most important example	last but not least		

Consult Appendix B for a complete list of transitions.

BUILDING SKILLS 4-4: Writing Topic Sentences for Examples

Circle the best topic sentence based on the listed supporting sentences.

1. Topic Sentences:
   a. Flowers are everywhere in our lives.
   b. In our lives, certain days, happy or sad, are often marked with flowers.

Supporting Sentences:
- Valentine's Day is about giving red or pink roses to loved ones.
- Mother's Day is about the multicolored bouquets of flowers given to mothers.
- Prom corsages are colorful flowers worn on the wrists of those attending a prom.
- Wedding flowers are used in the bride's bouquet and mark the color theme for the wedding ceremony.
- Funeral wreaths are white or red roses arranged in different shapes and used during a funeral ceremony.

2. Topic Sentences:
   a. The used car for sale has several advantageous features.
   b. The used car for sale is good.

Supporting Sentences:
- The engine is perfectly clean.
- It has low mileage.
- The interior is well kept.
- It has air bags.

Now, produce a clear illustration topic sentence and support sentences for each of the focused topics provided.

3. Focused Topic: Unattractive clothing styles
   Topic Sentence:

   _____

   _____

   Supporting Sentences:

   _____

   _____

   _____

   _____

4. Focused Topic: Rude behavior at restaurants
   Topic Sentence:

   _____

   _____

Supporting Sentences:

_____

_____

_____

_____

Development Sentences

Your examples will only be as good as the details you use in explaining them. Once you have chosen the three or more main examples you will discuss in your paragraph, you need to provide details that give more information about each example. Your details must be complete sentences that give clear, sufficient, and specific information about why and how each example relates to the topic sentence.

For each example, consider using different development sentences (or FRIEDs—facts, reasons, incidents, examples, or details). Try not to stick with one kind of development sentence for all your development sentences as that will limit your writing and bore your reader. Also, try not to over- or under- develop one supporting sentence more or less than the rest of the supporting sentences. Use roughly an equal amount of development sentences for each supporting sentence.

Consider how the example of helping cancer patients could be developed with facts, reasons, incidents, examples, and details. Here is what the development sentences could look like:

Lastly and most importantly, I would help cancer patients.	*Detail*
I would use my millions to start a company of "Healers	*Detail*
on Wheelers" to aid cancer patients with homecare and	*Reason*
I would employ my family members to help me run it,	*Detail*
so they all have jobs and can afford to go to college.	*Reason*
I would also donate half of the money from that company to	*Fact*
the Meals on Wheels charity that helps and feeds the sick	*Detail*
elderly and to cancer research to help cancer patients.	*Reason*
	Detail

Concluding Sentence

In most stand-alone paragraphs, a concluding sentence is encouraged and sometimes required. The concluding sentence may be optional if the illustration paragraph does not stand on its own when it is part of an essay. As the final sentence in the paragraph, the objective of the concluding sentence is to end the discussion; therefore, do not start a new idea; instead, close off your discussion by summarizing the supporting examples that reinforce the topic sentence.

Paying for my grandfather's healthcare, buying my parents their dream home, and helping cancer patients are three things I would do if I won the lottery.

Another way to conclude an illustration paragraph would be to offer a thoughtful observation or remark about the focused topic.

One thing I would do if I ever won a million-dollar lottery is help others including my grandfather, my parents, and cancer patients.

👆 MEMORY TIP

Remember these methods for formulating a concluding sentence:

- **R**estating
- **O**bserving
- **R**emarking
- **S**ummarizing

You can easily remember these methods by using the acronym RORS.

EXAMPLE OF AN ILLUSTRATION PARAGRAPH

Topic: television shows

Millions for Hope

As I sat thinking about the bad news I just heard from my Mom, I began to fantasize about how winning a ten million-dollar lottery would help. With this money, I would do several things that would help my loved ones and other people. The first thing I would do with my overnight millions is pay off the debt from the expensive healthcare my grandfather needs in his battle with cancer. My parents, aided by my grandfather's retirement money, have been paying for my grandfather's medical treatments and homecare. However, in the last three months, money has run out. If I became rich, I would pay off that debt and hire a full-time nurse to help with my grandfather's care. The second thing I would do with those millions is buy my parents a big house with all the upgrades, so they can enjoy their home without the worry of paying for it. They have worked so hard all their lives, and they deserve to re-lax in their dream home. Then, my parents will have more time to spend with my grandfather without the worry and fear over money. Lastly and most importantly, I would help cancer patients. I would use my millions to start a company of "Healers on Wheelers" to aid cancer patients with homecare, and I would employ my family members to help me run it, so they all would have jobs and can afford to go to college. I would also donate half of the money from that company to the Meals on Wheels charity that helps and feeds the sick elderly and to cancer research to help cancer patients. In the end, if I ever became an overnight lottery millionaire, I would pay for my grandfather's healthcare, buy my parents their dream home, and help cancer patients.

◗ BUILDING SKILLS TOGETHER 4-1: Evaluating an Illustration Paragraph

Working in a small group, read the following paragraph and answer the evaluation questions that follow.

Unplanned Time.doc

Unplanned Time

There are several obstacles to my pursuit of education. My first obstacle is money. Right now, I am receiving financial aid for my classes; however, books are very expensive. I work part-time only, and I do not make very much. After food, gas, and everyday expenses, there is not enough money left for school. I do not want to ask my parents for money; similarly, they are always short on money with having to take care of all four of their children and the house. My second obstacle is not having a major. I have changed my major four times because I have changed my mind on what I wanted to do or be in life. I took cosmetology classes before my general education classes, and I took classes that I really did not need; therefore, I have to spend more money and time now taking necessary prerequisite classes to graduate. My biggest obstacle is time. I have a license in cosmetology, and I want to work in a hair salon, but I do not have time because I am a full-time student. In the cosmetology business, I must be at the salon as much as possible in order to take walk-in clients, but with my full schedule at school and my full load of studying, I barely have an hour to myself let alone my clients. I have resolved to finish my classes, however long that takes, before working on my cosmetology career. Not having money, not having a plan, and not having time are three major obstacles to my pursuit of education.

1. Underline the topic sentence in the paragraph. Does it indicate the illustration pattern of writing? How? What might you change or add?

   _____

   _____

2. How many supporting sentences are in this paragraph? Write them down in the order they are discussed. How are they effective in explaining the topic sentence?

   _____

   _____

   _____

   _____

3. Circle the transition words. What order (time, space, or importance) is used to guide the reader from example to example? How effective are the transitions?

   _____

   _____

4. Underline all the development sentences (or FRIEDs); then, choose one of the development sentences from each supporting sentence, write it down, and state the kind of FRIED it is. Are there enough development sentences to explain each supporting idea?

   _____

   _____

   _____

   _____

5. State the concluding sentence. Identify the method (restating, observing, remarking, or summarizing) the writer uses to conclude the paragraph. Does the concluding sentence close off the paragraph or does it leave the reader hanging?

   _____

   _____

   _____

   _____

6. State the point of view (first, second, or third person) used in this paragraph. How effective is it for the writer's purpose? Is it used consistently throughout?

_____

_____

7. What do you think of the title? Is it catchy? Is it reflective of what the paragraph discusses?

_____

_____

SUGGESTED TOPICS FOR WRITING ILLUSTRATION PARAGRAPHS

Choose one of the following topics or use one of your own, and then use prewriting techniques to develop your draft for an illustration paragraph.

Books you like	Annoying work habits
Irritations at a movie theater	Desired or undesired jobs
Movies you like/dislike	Excuses for missing work/ bad performance
Creative hobbies	Challenges faced by older college students
Qualities of a great athlete	Peer pressure
The benefits of Twitter or Facebook	Rules at your workplace or home

BUILDING SKILLS TOGETHER 4-2: Illustration Paragraph Feedback Checklist

Once the rough draft of your illustration paragraph is completed, have a partner read it and answer the following revision and editing questions. You may also use this checklist to revise and edit your own paragraph.

Revising Paragraph Structure

☐ What is the topic sentence? What is the focused topic? How does the topic sentence indicate that illustration is the pattern used? What might you change or add?

☐ What examples are used as supporting sentences? How do they relate to the topic sentence? Are there enough sentences supporting the topic sentence? What might you change or add?

☐ Are clear transition words used to move you from one example to another? Do they show an order of importance? What might you change or add?

☐ Are sufficient development sentences (or FRIEDs) used for each example or supporting sentence? Where can you make improvements?

☐ How does the concluding sentence end the illustration paragraph? What concluding method (restating, observing, remarking, or summarizing) is used?

☐ What point of view is used in the illustration paragraph? How relevant is it to the writer's purpose? Is it consistent throughout the paragraph? Are any changes needed?

☐ Is there a title? Is it catchy and reflective of the illustration paragraph?

Editing Spelling, Diction, and Sentence Construction

☐ Are there any misspelled words?

☐ Are appropriate and specific words used?

☐ Are any slang words, text message language, or clichés used?

☐ Consider sentence structure and correct any errors with:

  ☐ Fragments, run-ons, and comma splices

  ☐ Misplaced or dangling modifiers

  ☐ Pronoun agreement

  ☐ Subject and verb agreement

Final Assessment

☐ What do you like the most about the paragraph?

☐ What are you unclear about or have difficulty with in this paragraph?

CHAPTER FIVE: Cause or Effect
Building Paragraphs
with Reasons or Results

Why is smoking bad for you? How dangerous is the flu? Why is math a required college course? How would a new finance procedure affect work performance? All these questions try to determine the causes or effects of an action or situation, and many college-level writing tasks require that you identify causes or effects for a variety of subjects.

Causes and effects are used to explain, show, or analyze a subject. A **cause** is what makes something happen. For example, a cause for pollution is fuel emissions from cars and industrial factories. An **effect** is what happens because of something. For example, an effect of pollution is lung cancer or respiratory allergies.

 MEMORY TIP

Other words for **cause** include *factor, reason, source, root,* and *basis.*

Other words for **effect** include *consequence, result, outcome,* and *product.*

Although you may use both causes *and* effects in your writing, it is best to focus on one or the other in a paragraph because it is easier to achieve unity and coherence. A cause or effect paragraph makes it clear whether causes or effects are the focus of the paragraph and uses specific, detailed, and real causes or effects as support.

BUILDING TIP

To understand **causes**, consider the <u>past</u> for reasons <u>why</u> something happened.

To understand **effects**, consider the <u>future</u> for possible <u>consequences</u> of an action.

WRITING A CAUSE OR EFFECT PARAGRAPH

In using this pattern, your purpose is to give your readers an analysis of causes for or effects of your subject. In fact, the causes or effects that you explain are the actual supporting sentences in your paragraph, so choose them well. Begin your writing with some prewriting activities that will help you reflect on causes or effects about your subject. One useful prewriting technique for this pattern is listing. As you are prewriting, be sure to draw on causes or effects that fit the following characteristics:

- Causes or effects are real, logical, and believable to the reader.
- Causes or effects are directly related and important to the subject.

When you are writing about causes, be careful that you do not include a cause just because it happened beforehand; sometimes coincidence sways the analysis. For example, the fact that you had chocolate cake last night at dinner does not mean it is the reason why you got an upset stomach the next day. Likewise, use the same caution when writing about effects: do not confuse something that

 BUILDING TIP

There is a difference between an actual cause and a **contributing factor**. A cause is a direct and definitive reason for something to happen.

A causes B.

Fuel emissions cause pollution.

However, a contributing factor *may* be one of many reasons for something to happen. When you include contributing factors, you use qualifiers (or restricting words such as *often, at times...*).

A *may, might, sometimes,* or *can* be the cause for B.

Car fuel emissions, among many other things, may cause pollution.

When you state your causes, be careful how you state them because the meaning shifts depending on the language or qualifiers you use.

happens after something else with the effect. Getting an upset stomach the next day was not an effect of eating chocolate cake at dinner last night.

Consider the subject, divorce, for a cause or effect paragraph. In your prewriting, write down your subject, then on the left side list as many reasons for divorce and on the right side list as many effects of divorce. Then, look at your lists.

Causes   (Divorce)   Effects
money issues   loneliness/depression
adultery   betrayal
children issues   custody battles
abuse   insecurity
lack of love   social adjustment
loss of job   financial problems

Which side appeals more to you? Which side are you more comfortable developing? Decide on that first; then, isolate the reasons you feel are most logical, believable, and important in your list. Be sure that in selecting the main reasons, you are comfortable presenting and discussing them for the reader. Suppose you picked as your topic causes for divorce, you could consider the following three reasons (you may pick more):

■ money issues
■ adultery
■ children issues

Decide on which cause is the most important; there is no right way to this. It depends on you, the writer, what you find or consider the most important reason or effect, but for this example, you may order your reasons as follows: money issues, children issues, and adultery. Now, you are ready to start your rough draft.

GENERIC PLAN FOR CAUSE OR EFFECT PARAGRAPH

Topic Sentence: Focused Topic + Causes or Effects
    Supporting Sentence 1: Cause 1 or Effect 1
        Development Sentences (or FRIEDs)
    Supporting Sentence 2: Cause 2 or Effect 2
        Development Sentences (or FRIEDs)
    Supporting Sentence 3: Cause 3 or Effect 3 (Most important cause or effect)
        Development Sentences (or FRIEDs)
Concluding Sentence

BUILDING SKILLS 5-1: Listing Causes and Effects

Use the following topics to brainstorm lists of causes and effects, then circle three causes or three effects to focus on for the topic.

1. Text messaging
   Causes   Effects
   _____   _____
   _____   _____
   _____   _____
   _____   _____
   _____   _____
   _____   _____
   _____   _____
   _____   _____

2. Interviewing for a job
   Causes   Effects
   _____   _____
   _____   _____
   _____   _____
   _____   _____
   _____   _____
   _____   _____
   _____   _____

3. Marriage
   Causes   Effects
   _____   _____
   _____   _____
   _____   _____
   _____   _____
   _____   _____
   _____   _____
   _____   _____
   _____   _____

Topic Sentence

The topic sentence in a cause or effect paragraph clearly states the focused topic and indicates whether causes or effects will be discussed. Use words like *reasons, effects, results,* and *factors* in your topic sentence and word it so that the reader knows you are discussing the causes for or effects of your focused topic.

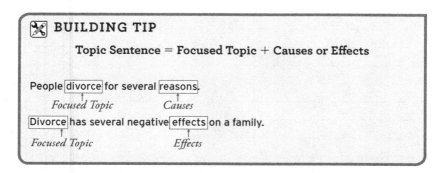

⚒ BUILDING TIP

Topic Sentence = Focused Topic + Causes or Effects

People ⟨divorce⟩ for several ⟨reasons⟩.
    Focused Topic   *Causes*
⟨Divorce⟩ has several negative ⟨effects⟩ on a family.
Focused Topic   *Effects*

BUILDING SKILLS 5-2: Recognizing Effective Cause or Effect Topic Sentences

Read each sentence and write *TS* next to the ones that are effective cause or effect topic sentences, and *X* next to those that are not effective topic sentences.

_____ 1. Pollution produces several harmful consequences.

_____ 2. Binge drinking is everywhere.

_____ 3. There are several factors that lead business leaders to fail at managing their corporations.

_____ 4. It is not hard to explain the benefit of college.

_____ 5. The iPhone is a huge success due to several important reasons.

_____ 6. Unemployment can result in many social problems.

_____ 7. Teen pregnancy can have negative effects.

_____ 8. Professional athletes have high salaries.

_____ 9. For a number of reasons, I gained weight at an alarming rate.

_____ 10. Credit cards lure you into spending more money.

BUILDING SKILLS 5-3: Writing Cause or Effect Topic Sentences

On a separate sheet of paper, prewrite for each topic; then, write a strong topic sentence for each topic with a clear cause or effect focus.

1. Writing

   _____

   _____

2. Study skills

   _____

   _____

3. Home cooking

   _____

   _____

4. Time management

   _____

   _____

5. Siblings

   _____

   _____

Supporting Sentences

In cause or effect paragraphs, support is made up of the causes or effects chosen to explain the topic sentence. You may choose as many as you want; however, a generally accepted practice is to choose three to five. Your supporting sentences are usually created from the ideas you identify in your prewriting. Supporting sentences help you explain your topic sentence. For the topic sentence about divorce, the supporting sentences may be about money issues, children issues, and adultery. Supporting sentences for this pattern are usually organized by order of importance, saving the most important or intense cause or effect for last in order to create a strong impression on the reader. Be sure to use transitions to move the reader from one cause or effect to another.

TRANSITIONS USED IN CAUSE OR EFFECT PARAGRAPHS

Common transitions used in cause or effect paragraphs are:

first cause, second cause, most important cause
one cause, another cause, most contributing cause
one effect, another effect, most damaging effect

Consult Appendix B for a complete list of transitions.

Development Sentences

The specific information or the facts, reasons, incidents, examples, and details that you use to explain or show each cause or effect must be chosen carefully. Remember to use roughly an equal amount of development sentences (or FRIEDs) for each cause or effect, so you do not over- or under-develop your ideas. Development sentences for the supporting idea of money as a cause for divorce may include an example of a couple fighting over money matters or an incident where money played a big role in divorce.

Concluding Sentence

For a stand-alone cause or effect paragraph, the concluding sentence ends the discussion and does not start a new idea. One way you may consider concluding your paragraph is by summarizing the supporting sentences to reinforce the focused topic or by restating the topic sentence.

> Money issues, children issues, and adultery are three causes for many divorces.

Another way to write the concluding sentence in a cause or effect paragraph would be to offer a thoughtful remark about the focused topic.

> Regardless of the reasons for it, divorce is a hurtful process to go through.

EXAMPLE OF A CAUSE OR EFFECT PARAGRAPH

Topic: divorce

Grounds for Divorce

Many marriages thrive over the years, but occasionally some falter and end up in divorce. The most noted reasons for divorce include money issues, children issues, and sadly adultery. One reason for divorce is money issues.

The spending habits of one spouse might affect the delicate makeup of a marriage. For example, my divorced friend, Stephanie, loved to spend money even though she and her ex-husband were on a budget. Her ex-husband always complained that she was the reason for their debt, until one day he walked out on her and left her to deal with the debt. Another reason for divorce is children issues. Many times, spouses disagree on how to discipline or treat their children. This disagreement sometimes leads to tension and fights in a marriage. For example, Daisy and Jonas divorced because she claimed he was too harsh with the children, and he claimed she was too lenient with them. The most significant reason for divorce is adultery. Adultery is a betrayal of the vows of commitment. Lilia caught her husband cheating on her with one of her girlfriends. With her built-in cell phone camera, she took a picture of him with the other woman and used that picture as grounds for her divorce and settlement case. Sadly, money issues, children issues, and adultery are several reasons why some marriages end in divorce.

BUILDING SKILLS TOGETHER 5-1: Evaluating a Cause or Effect Paragraph

Working in a small group, read the following paragraph and answer the evaluation questions that follow.

Overindulgence.doc

Overindulgence

There are several effects of drug and alcohol abuse. The first effect of drug and alcohol abuse is acting in a criminal way. While under the influence of these substances, a person might do or say things he or she does not really mean. For example, my drug-addicted cousin would go to any length to get his "fix"; he would tell lies on top of lies and steal money or saleable things from anyone. The second effect of drug and alcohol abuse is loss of one's well-being. When a person abuses drugs and alcohol, he or she stops caring about his or her health and may not eat or sleep well. As a result, the skin turns pale and unhealthy, the eyes become feverish and empty, and the body becomes a skeleton. Some drug addicts, like my cousin, would rather spend money on the next fix than on clean clothes, so he walks around with foul body odor. The worst effect of drug and alcohol abuse is overdosing. The amounts of alcohol or drugs needed for each "fix" increases the more a person indulges. At some point, overindulging causes overdosing where blood poisoning, liver damage, or brain damage set in. As the body shuts down from trying to absorb the massive quantity at one time, the heart stops, and the person, like my cousin, dies. Acting in criminal ways, losing one's well-being, and possibly overdosing are three significant effects that may happen from drug or alcohol abuse.

1. Underline the topic sentence in the paragraph. Does it indicate the cause or effect pattern of writing? How? What might you change or add?

   _____

   _____

2. How many supporting sentences are in this paragraph? Write them down in the order they are discussed. How are they effective in explaining the topic sentence?

   _____

   _____

   _____

   _____

3. Circle the transition words. What order (time, space, or importance) is used to guide the reader from point to point? How effective are the transitions?

   _____

   _____

4. Underline all the development sentences (or FRIEDs); then, choose one of the development sentences from each supporting sentence in the paragraph, write it down, and state the kind of FRIED it is. Are there enough development sentences to explain each supporting idea?

   _____

   _____

   _____

   _____

5. State the concluding sentence. Identify the method (restating, observing, remarking, or summarizing) the writer uses to conclude the paragraph. Does the concluding sentence close off the paragraph or does it leave the reader hanging?

_____

_____

_____

_____

6. State the point of view (first, second, or third person) used in this paragraph. Is it effective for the writer's purpose? Is it used consistently throughout?

_____

_____

7. What do you think of the title? Is it catchy? Is it reflective of what the paragraph discusses?

_____

_____

SUGGESTED TOPICS FOR WRITING CAUSE OR EFFECT PARAGRAPHS

Choose one of the following topics or use one of your own, and then use prewriting techniques to develop your draft for a cause or effect paragraph.

Having a pet	Harassment
Cosmetic surgery	Whistle-blowing
Success	Participating in team sports
Road rage/aggressive driving	Dropping out of school/college
Rude neighbors	Credit cards
Rude neighbors	Substance abuse

BUILDING SKILLS TOGETHER 5-2: Cause or Effect Paragraph Feedback Checklist

Once the rough draft of your cause or effect paragraph is completed, have a partner read it and answer the following revision and editing questions. You may also use this checklist to revise and edit your own paragraph.

Revising Paragraph Structure

☐ What is the topic sentence? What is the focused topic? How does the topic sentence indicate that cause or effect is the pattern used? What might you change or add?

☐ What causes (or effects) are used as supporting sentences? How do they relate to the topic sentence? Are there enough sentences supporting the topic sentence? What might you change or add?

☐ Are clear transition words used to move you from one cause (or effect) to another? Do they show an order of importance? What might you change or add?

☐ Are sufficient development sentences (or FRIEDs) used for each cause (or effect) or supporting sentence? Where can you make improvements?

☐ How does the concluding sentence end the cause (or effect) discussion? What concluding method (restating, observing, remarking, or summarizing) is used?

☐ What point of view is used in the cause (or effect) paragraph? How relevant is it to the writer's purpose? Is it consistent throughout the paragraph? Are any changes needed?

☐ Is there a title? Is it catchy and reflective of the cause (or effect) discussion?

Editing Spelling, Diction, and Sentence Construction

☐ Are there any misspelled words?

☐ Are appropriate and specific words used?

☐ Are any slang words, text message language, or clichés used?

☐ Consider sentence structure and correct any errors with:

    ☐ Fragments, run-ons, and comma splices

    ☐ Misplaced or dangling modifiers

    ☐ Pronoun agreement

    ☐ Subject and verb agreement

Final Assessment

☐ What do you like the most about this paragraph?

☐ What are you unclear about or have difficulty with in this paragraph?

CHAPTER SIX: Classification
Building Paragraphs with Groups

You may organize your clothes closet into sections for T-shirts, shorts, pants, shirts, sweats, socks, and shoes. Or, you may organize your refrigerator into a dairy section, a vegetable section, a meat section, a beverage section, and a condiment section. In some college classes, you may be required to write paragraph assignments that organize or classify discipline-specific subjects.

Classification groups ideas, things, or people into categories or classes. It shows different classes of the same subject. Consider a grocery store. It has different areas of focus: produce area, meat area, frozen foods area, dairy food area, and so on. Each area has a designated focus to make it easier for the shopper to find everything. However, each category is independent of the others or in a class by itself.

WRITING A CLASSIFICATION PARAGRAPH

To classify, start with a grouping principle that is the basis to sort the topic into groups or classes. A single grouping principle is the overall organizing idea you use to look at the subject in order to group it into separate groups or classes. In other words, it is *how* you view the subject. Apply that principle to establish at least three useful groups or classes, and be aware that the grouping principle is the one common characteristic that unites the different groups or classes. Last, fully explain each group or class.

When you use classification as a pattern of writing, remember these basic guidelines:

- Use a single grouping principle to sort the subject.
- Establish useful groups or classes that have the grouping principle as a common feature.

- Ensure that your groups do not overlap.
- Fully explain each group or class.

Here is a visual representation of the classification process:

Topic: Restaurants
Grouping principle: Location
Groups/classes: Stadium restaurants
                          Resort restaurants
                          Airport restaurants

Explanation of each group/class:

- Stadium restaurants are located inside stadiums or big sportscenters. They are fast-food restaurants that cater to spectators.
- Resort restaurants are located in hotels or in touristy areas and supply food to vacationers or recreation-minded people.
- Airport restaurants supply food to the air travelers while they wait for their flights. They have limited services because most airport restaurants are self-service, which means customers have to clean their tables after they finish their meals.

You can try several grouping principles on a given subject until you find the one you like or are comfortable using in your writing. Here is another way to classify restaurants:

Topic: Restaurants
Grouping principle: Letter grades for sanitation and food safety
Groups/classes: Letter A restaurants—Excellent sanitation and food safety
                          Letter B restaurants—Acceptable sanitation and food safety
                          Letter C restaurants—Minimal sanitation and food safety

Explanation of each group/class:

- A *Letter A* restaurant is one that makes cleanliness a priority, so it has minimal violations related to sanitation and food handling.
- A *Letter B* restaurant is one that has several violations related to sanitation and food handling and will need to be reinspected after improvements.
- A *Letter C* restaurant is in serious violation of sanitary and food handling guidelines and may be required to suspend operation until clear improvements are made.

As you designate your groups or classes, discard easy or impractical phrasing such as *good/bad/average* or *slow/medium/fast*, or *beautiful/plain/ugly* as the groups will overlap, and you will find that your explanation of each group is bland and brief.

Consider supermarket shoppers as a subject for classification. Start your prewriting; listing or clustering works best for this pattern. Although there are different ways to look at this topic, here is one way to consider it:

Topic:	Supermarket shoppers
Grouping principle:	Attitudes while shopping
Groups/classes:	Purposeful shoppers
	Leisurely shoppers
	Bored shoppers
	Lost and confused shoppers

You could discuss all four classes, or you could narrow down your discussion. Of the four classes, suppose you decide to focus on purposeful, leisurely, and lost or confused shoppers as possible groups. Now you are ready to write your rough draft.

GENERIC PLAN FOR A CLASSIFICATION PARAGRAPH

Topic Sentence: Focused Topic + Grouping Principle + Categories
    Supporting Sentence 1: Group 1
        Development Sentences (or FRIEDs)
    Supporting Sentence 2: Group 2
        Development Sentences (or FRIEDs)
    Supporting Sentence 3: Group 3
        Development Sentences (or FRIEDs)
Concluding Sentence

BUILDING SKILLS 6-1: Using Grouping Principles

For each topic that follows, one of the categories does not fit the same grouping principle as the rest. Underline the one that does not fit and write the grouping principle on the line.

1. Topic:	Movies
Groups/Classes:	Comedy
	Author's name
	Horror
	Drama
Grouping Principle:	_____

2. Topic: Shoes
    Group/Classes: Running
                           Bowling
                           High heels
                           Golfing

    Grouping Principle: _____

3. Topic: Animals
    Groups/Classes: Cats
                           Dolphins
                           Dogs
                           Hamsters

    Grouping Principle: _____

BUILDING SKILL 6-2: Choosing Useful Categories

For the given topic and grouping principle, list two more useful groups/classes.

1. Topic: dates
   Grouping Principle: public location where date is held
       Group 1: restaurant date
       Group 2: _____
       Group 3: _____

2. Topic: friends
   Grouping Principle: degree of involvement
       Group 1: best friends—heavily involved
       Group 2: _____
       Group 3: _____

3. Topic: doctors
   Grouping Principle: motive for profession
       Group 1: interest in science
       Group 2: _____
       Group 3: _____

4. Topic: airline tickets
   Grouping Principle: passenger seating
       Group 1: first class
       Group 2: _____
       Group 3: _____

Topic Sentence

The topic sentence in a classification paragraph should indicate the focused topic and the grouping principle. There are several ways to state a classification topic sentence.

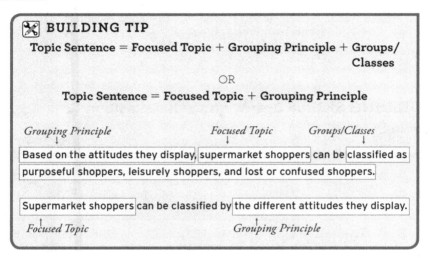

> **🔧 BUILDING TIP**
>
> Topic Sentence = Focused Topic + Grouping Principle + Groups/Classes
>
> OR
>
> Topic Sentence = Focused Topic + Grouping Principle
>
> *Grouping Principle*   *Focused Topic*   *Groups/Classes*
>
> Based on the attitudes they display, supermarket shoppers can be classified as purposeful shoppers, leisurely shoppers, and lost or confused shoppers.
>
> Supermarket shoppers can be classified by the different attitudes they display.
> *Focused Topic*   *Grouping Principle*

BUILDING SKILLS 6-3: Recognizing Classification Topic Sentences

Read each sentence and write *TS* next to the ones that are effective classification topic sentences and *X* next to those that are not effective classification topic sentences.

_____ 1. I have three bosses in my life.

_____ 2. Shoppers can be sorted into four categories based on their reasons for shopping.

_____ 3. Athletes are in different classes.

_____ 4. Drivers can be grouped into three groups by the makes of the cars they drive.

_____ 5. There are two types of teachers.

_____ 6. Depending on their yard upkeep, my neighbors can be classified into four different types.

_____ 7. Liars are in a class of their own.

_____ 8. Friends come in many shapes and sizes.

_____ 9. Human faces can be shaped in four ways.

_____ 10. Community college students can be classified by their academic intentions.

BUILDING SKILLS 6-4: Writing Classification
Topic Sentences

Prewrite and find a grouping principle for each topic. Then, on the lines that follow each topic, write a strong topic sentence with a clear classification focus.

1. Success

   _____

   _____

2. Fast food

   _____

   _____

3. Exercise routines

   _____

   _____

4. Smartphones

   _____

   _____

5. Dancers

   _____

   _____

Supporting Sentences

In classification, your individual groups or classes are the supporting sentences for your paragraph. Arrange the groups/classes logically and ensure that you do not have groups/classes that fall into a scale of good/average/bad or high/medium/low. Every group/class must be distinct and useful. There is no order of importance in a classification paragraph, so you are at liberty to place your groups/classes in any order you want as long as you have useful and distinct groups.

From the previous prewrite on supermarket shoppers, the supporting sentences are in this order: first, purposeful shoppers; second, the leisurely shoppers; and third, the lost and confused shoppers.

TRANSITIONS USED IN CLASSIFICATION PARAGRAPHS

one group	first kind	one class	one category
another group	second kind	another class	second category
third group	third kind	third class	last category

Consult Appendix B for a complete list of transitions.

Development Sentences

For each group or class, readers need specific examples, detail, and facts. Be sure to use a variety of development sentences (or FRIEDs) to make each group/class clear for your readers, and be sure to use roughly an equal amount of development sentences for each group or class. From the previous prewriting on shoppers, a FRIED for each one of the supporting sentences could be how they approach the task of shopping.

Concluding Sentence

The objective of the concluding sentence is to end the discussion; therefore, the concluding sentence in a classification paragraph should offer a thoughtful observation or remark about the classification. Remember not to start a new idea; instead, close off your discussion.

While the purposeful, leisurely, and lost or confused shoppers are interesting to watch, they all come to the supermarket for one thing or another.

Another way to write the concluding sentence would be to restate the supporting groups and the grouping principle.

Based on their attitudes, supermarket shoppers can be categorized as purposeful, leisurely, and lost or confused.

EXAMPLE OF A CLASSIFICATION PARAGRAPH

Topic: supermarket shoppers

Market Shoppers

Supermarket shoppers can be classified according to their attitudes while shopping. The first category is the purposeful shopper. Purposeful shoppers are intent and organized. They are short on time, so they stride in the store purposefully and walk directly to the appropriate aisle(s). They get what they need, and they get out of the store quickly. The second type of shopper is the leisurely shopper who enjoys strolling along getting pleasure from viewing all the different items that can be purchased or displayed. It is somewhat of a pastime for them, so they are the ones who amble down every aisle in the store. The last category is the lost and confused shopper. These shoppers walk down one aisle, look around, then turn back to go to another aisle. They usually repeat this process a few times before they ask for help from a sales associate or use their cell phones to call for directions, usually from the person that sent them in to shop to begin with. These shoppers do not like supermarkets and only come if they absolutely have to. While the purposeful, leisurely, and lost or confused shoppers are interesting to watch, they all must come to the supermarket for one thing or another.

◆ BUILDING SKILLS TOGETHER 6-1: Evaluating a Classification Paragraph

Working in a small group, read the following paragraph and answer the evaluation questions that follow.

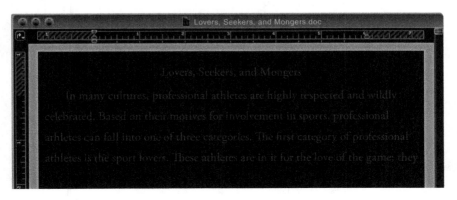

are passionate about the sport's principles and setups. They are highly skilled at playing the sport, but they do it to be a part of the sport, not for the personal or professional advantages it could bring them. The second category of professional athletes is the fame-seekers. These athletes push themselves so hard for so long to create a reputation and a name for themselves. They are the ones who want to be in the Hall of Fame. The third category of professional athletes is the money mongers. These highly skilled and talented athletes are in the sport for the money they can make from it. A professional athlete's estimated yearly salary is between $2 to $25 million. A few years of playing professionally will allow that athlete to live a rich and comfortable life. The motive for involvement in sports produces professional athletes that may be sport lovers, fame-seekers, or money mongers.

1. Underline the topic sentence in the paragraph. Does it indicate the classification pattern of writing? What is the grouping principle? What might you change or add?

   _____

   _____

2. How many supporting sentences or groups are in this classification paragraph? Write them down in the order they are discussed. How are they effective in explaining the topic sentence?

   _____

   _____

   _____

   _____

3. Circle the transition words. What order (time, space, or importance) is used to guide the reader from point to point? How effective are the transitions?

   _____

   _____

4. Underline all the development sentences (or FRIEDs); then, choose one of the development sentences from each supporting sentence in the

paragraph, write it down, and state the kind of FRIED it is. Are there enough development sentences to explain each supporting idea?

_____

_____

_____

_____

5. State the concluding sentence. Identify the method (restating, observing, remarking, or summarizing) the writer uses to conclude the paragraph. Does the concluding sentence close off the paragraph or does it leave the reader hanging?

_____

_____

_____

_____

6. State the point of view (first, second, or third person) used in this paragraph. Is it effective for the writer's purpose? Is it used consistently throughout?

_____

_____

7. What do you think of the title? Is it catchy? Is it reflective of what the paragraph discusses?

_____

_____

SUGGESTED TOPICS FOR WRITING CLASSIFICATION PARAGRAPHS

Choose one of the following topics or use one of your own and then use prewriting techniques to develop your draft for a classification paragraph.

Junk foods	Students in a college class
Popular music	Assignments in a college class
Goals	Bosses
Professional athletes	Workers or employees
Pet owners	Clothing styles
Diets	Popular websites
eReader devices	Drivers

● BUILDING SKILLS TOGETHER 6-2: Classification
Paragraph Feedback Checklist

Once the rough draft of your classification paragraph is completed, have a partner read it and answer the following revision and editing questions. You may also use this checklist to revise and edit your own paragraph.

Revising Paragraph Structure

☐ What is the topic sentence? What is the focused topic? How does the topic sentence indicate that classification is the pattern used? What might you change or add?

☐ What groups are used as supporting sentences? How do they relate to the topic sentence? Are there enough sentences supporting the topic sentence? What might you change or add?

☐ Are clear transition words used to move you from one group to another? Do they show an order of importance? What might you change or add?

☐ Are sufficient development sentences (or FRIEDs) used for each group or supporting sentence? Where can you make improvements?

☐ How does the concluding sentence end the classification paragraph? What concluding method (restating, observing, remarking, or summarizing) is used?

☐ What point of view is used in the classification paragraph? How relevant is it to the writer's purpose? Is it consistent throughout the paragraph? Are any changes needed?

☐ Is there a title? Is it catchy and reflective of the classification paragraph?

Editing Spelling, Diction, and Sentence Construction

☐ Are there any misspelled words?

☐ Are appropriate and specific words used?

☐ Are any slang words, text message language, or clichés used?

☐ Consider the sentence structure and correct any errors with:

　☐ Fragments, run-ons, and comma splices

　☐ Misplaced or dangling modifiers

☐ Pronoun agreement

☐ Subject and verb agreement

Final Assessment

☐ What do you like the most about this paragraph?

☐ What are you unclear about or have difficulty with in this paragraph?

CHAPTER SEVEN: Comparison or Contrast
Building Paragraphs with Similarities or Differences

Does Middle Town College offer similar programs to American Community College? If not, how are they different? Does the new Flip camera offer similar benefits to the one you have? Many of us comparison shop to determine similarities and differences or pros and cons before we do something or spend money. In many college courses, like psychology, history, business, or chemistry, you may be asked to write a comparison or contrast analysis on discipline-specific subjects.

When you write a comparison or contrast paragraph, you show how two people, two places, two things, or two ideas are similar or different. You place the topics next to each other to evaluate the similarities or differences. **Comparison** means to compare and shows the similarities between two topics, whereas **contrast** shows the differences. Generally, the word *compare* is used to mean compare or contrast, but in this book, *compare* means only to compare. However, check with your instructor, as each discipline has its own requirements.

WRITING A COMPARISON OR CONTRAST PARAGRAPH
To write a comparison or contrast paragraph, choose two topics that can be comparable or have something in common, so you can develop points of comparison or contrast. An example of two comparable topics could be cars and motorcycles because both are a means of transportation but with different features. Once you have selected your topics, follow these steps:

1. Decide on the focus or purpose you want to emphasize: similarities or differences.
2. List points of similarities or differences between the two topics.

3. Select several similarities or differences to use as supporting sentences.
4. Organize in order the points of similarity or difference.

You can choose two different orders when writing a comparison or contrast paragraph: the **point-by-point** (PBP) order or the **topic-by-topic** (TBT) order.

POINT-BY-POINT (PBP)	TOPIC-BY-TOPIC (TBT)
Topic Sentence	Topic Sentence
Point 1	Topic A
Topic A	Point 1
Development Sentences (or FRIEDs)	Development Sentences (or FRIEDs)
Topic B	Point 2
Development Sentences (or FRIEDs)	Development Sentences (or FRIEDs)
Point 2	Point 3
Topic A	Development Sentences (or FRIEDs)
Development Sentences (or FRIEDs)	Topic B
Topic B	Point 1
Development Sentences (or FRIEDs)	Development Sentences (or FRIEDs)
Point 3	Point 2
Topic A	Development Sentences (or FRIEDs)
Development Sentences (or FRIEDs)	Point 3
Topic B	Development Sentences (or FRIEDs)
Development Sentences (or FRIEDs)	
Concluding Sentence	Concluding Sentence

The point-by-point (PBP) order presents one point of similarity or difference at a time about both topics and then moves to the next point. It is better suited for college writing and will be the focus of this chapter. The topic-by-topic (TBT) order presents all the points about the first topic and then all the points about the second topic.

Consider the following topics for a comparison/contrast paragraph: online and traditional classrooms. Listing often works best as a prewriting technique for this pattern of writing. In listing similarities and differences between the two topics, we may get the following:

Online and Traditional Classrooms

Similarities	Differences
Same material is taught	Flexibility in scheduling
Same assignments is given	Location
Course planned by instructor	Student-teacher interactions
Same amount of study time	Technology needs/expertise

BUILDING SKILLS 7-1: Finding Points of Similarity or Contrast

Under each topic, list two similarities and two differences; then, choose which side you would focus on.

1. Topics: basketball and football

   Similarities   Differences

   _____   _____

   _____   _____

   _____   _____

            Focus: _____

2. Topics: Mexican food and Chinese food

   Similarities   Differences

   _____   _____

   _____   _____

   _____   _____

            Focus: _____

3. Topics: dancing and singing

   Similarities   Differences

   _____   _____

   _____   _____

   _____   _____

            Focus: _____

4. Topics: men's and women's communication

Similarities   Differences

_____   _____

_____   _____

_____   _____

Focus: _____

5. Topics: Thanksgiving and Fourth of July holidays

Similarities   Differences

_____   _____

_____   _____

_____   _____

Focus: _____

Topic Sentence

The topic sentence in a comparison or contrast paragraph includes the focused topic of whether the two topics are similar or different. You should state it in your own words and style of writing as long as you indicate the focus of whether the two topics are similar or different. Be careful not to state that one topic is better because that is the argumentation pattern of writing instead of the comparison or contrast pattern.

> **⚒ BUILDING TIP**
>
> **Topic Sentence = Focused topic that shows Topic A and Topic B are similar**
>
> Online and traditional classes offer students several similar benefits.
>
> **Topic Sentence = Focused topic that shows Topic A and Topic B are different**
>
> Online and traditional classes are significantly different in several ways.

BUILDING SKILLS 7-2: Recognizing Comparison or Contrast Topic Sentences

Read each sentence and write *TS* next to the ones that are effective comparison or contrast topic sentences and *X* next to those that are not effective comparison or contrast topic sentences.

_____ 1. There are major differences between soccer and football.

_____ 2. Fast food is better than home cooking.

_____ 3. There are several similarities between my father and grandfather.

_____ 4. Dog owners are a different breed than cat owners.

_____ 5. Laptops are not that useful.

_____ 6. I have a different lifestyle today than I did ten years ago.

_____ 7. My language at home is worse than my language at work.

_____ 8. My construction job is different from my singing job.

_____ 9. There are several similarities between the roles of males in the Mexican and Middle Eastern cultures.

_____ 10. Neat people are meaner than sloppy people.

BUILDING SKILLS 7-3: Writing Comparison or Contrast Topic Sentences

Prewrite for each topic and on the lines below write a strong topic sentence with a clear comparison or contrast focus for each topic.

1. Two vacations

   _____

   _____

2. Two influential people

   _____

   _____

3. Two restaurants

   _____

   _____

4. Living with family and living alone

   _____

   _____

5. Skateboarders and snowboarders

   _____

   _____

Supporting Sentences

The supporting sentences in a comparison or contrast paragraph are selected from the points of similarities or points of differences that you listed in brainstorming for the two topics. You can present and develop the supporting sentences either by using point-by-point order or topic-by-topic order, although the preferred method for college writing is point-by-point order. There is no order of importance in a comparison or contrast paragraph so long as the points are organized in a logical manner. Working with the topic of differences between online and traditional classes, you would focus on several points of differences as the supporting sentences. The supporting sentences might look like this:

Supporting sentence 1: **The first difference between online and traditional classes is convenience of scheduling.**

Supporting sentence 2: **The second difference between online and traditional classes is Internet dependency.**

Supporting sentence 3: **The third difference between online and traditional classes is person-to-person interactions.**

TRANSITIONS USED IN COMPARISON OR CONTRAST PARAGRAPHS

one similarity	another similarity	a third similarity		
one difference	another difference	a third difference		
similarly	likewise	like	both	however
in contrast	unlike	while	on the other hand	
in comparison	nevertheless	whereas	on the contrary	

Consult Appendix B for a complete list of transitions.

Development Sentences

Each point of similarity (or difference) needs to have development sentences that show how Topic A then Topic B relates to each point of similarity (or difference). You decide the order of the topics, but whatever you choose to have as Topic A for the first point of similarity (or difference), you should use it as Topic A for all subsequent points of similarity (or difference). This consistency is crucial, so readers do not get confused about which topic you are discussing. Be sure to use a variety of development sentences (or FRIEDs) for each of the topics. Using the example of online and traditional classes, your development would look like this:

First difference is scheduling
Online classes (*Topic A*):	Development sentences (or FRIEDs)
Traditional classes *(Topic B)*:	Development sentences (or FRIEDs)

Second difference is Internet dependency
Online classes (*Topic A*):	Development sentences (or FRIEDs)
Traditional classes *(Topic B)*:	Development sentences (or FRIEDs)

Third difference is interactions
Online classes (*Topic A*):	Development sentences (or FRIEDs)
Traditional classes *(Topic B)*:	Development sentences (or FRIEDs)

The first difference between online and traditional courses is the convenience in scheduling. In an online course, students can schedule their college work at convenient times from the comforts of home. On the other hand, students in traditional courses must attend a physical classroom at specific times. — *Topic A* — *FRIED 1* — *Topic B* — *FRIED 1*

⚒ BUILDING TIP

If you do not use enough specific information or FRIEDs for development in the point-by-point order, the readers may experience a mechanical "ping-pong" effect that makes your writing boring. To avoid that, develop each supporting sentence thoroughly with enough development sentences.

Concluding Sentence

The objective of the concluding sentence is to end the discussion; therefore, the concluding sentence in a comparison or contrast paragraph should summarize the supporting sentences that reinforce the focused topic of comparison or contrast. Remember not to start a new idea; instead, close off your discussion.

Convenience of scheduling, Internet dependency, and person-to-person interactions are several differences between online and traditional classes. Another way to present the concluding sentence in a comparison or contrast paragraph would be to offer an insightful remark that reinforces the focused topic.

College students must carefully consider which course best fits their needs because online and traditional courses offer different learning experiences.

EXAMPLE OF A COMPARISON OR CONTRAST PARAGRAPH

Topic: contrasting online and traditional courses

Online or Offline Courses

In college, an online course is different from a traditional course. The first difference between online and traditional courses is the convenience in scheduling. In an online course, students can schedule their college work at convenient times around other commitments such as full-time jobs or childcare. Class can be attended at any time from the comforts of home. On the other hand, students in traditional courses must attend a physical classroom at specific times. A second difference between online and traditional courses is Internet dependency. An online course relies exclusively on a reliable Internet connection because students and teachers connect virtually via e-mail or discussion boards to discuss course material or to submit assignments. In a traditional course, however, most of the discussion and assignment submission takes place "off-line" or in a brick-and-mortar classroom, so Internet dependency is not an issue. The final difference between online and traditional courses is the person-to-person interaction. In an online course, students never come into physical contact with the teacher or their classmates, so learning happens in isolation. On the other hand, in traditional courses, students interact in person with others, so students can connect with the teacher and classmates. College students must carefully consider the type of course that best fits their needs because online and traditional courses offer different learning experiences.

❚ BUILDING SKILLS TOGETHER 7-1: Evaluating a Comparison or Contrast Paragraph

Working in a small group, read the following paragraph and answer the evaluation questions that follow.

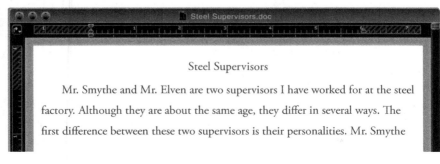

Steel Supervisors

Mr. Smythe and Mr. Elven are two supervisors I have worked for at the steel factory. Although they are about the same age, they differ in several ways. The first difference between these two supervisors is their personalities. Mr. Smythe is a highly organized, serious man. He is always concerned with reducing project costs and increasing profit numbers. On the other hand, Mr. Elven is a disorganized man who often loses his track of thought or misplaces log sheets yet cares about the profit numbers. In addition, my two supervisors differ in their management strategies. Mr. Smythe likes to keep us busy with many big projects and daily status reports. He needs to know every little project move, which encourages us to finish some projects ahead of schedule. On the other hand, Mr. Elven assigns projects randomly and likes monthly updates. He does not care how we accomplish the projects as long as we complete them by the deadline. The third difference between my two supervisors is their interactions with employees. Mr. Smythe is often in his office with the door closed. Occasionally, he walks around our cubicles, but otherwise he keeps to himself. Mr. Elven rarely sits at his cluttered office desk, and he is always in conversation with whoever has time for him. Mr. Smythe and Mr. Elven are two different steel factory supervisors, yet, in their own ways, they are effective at accomplishing their tasks.

1. Underline the topic sentence in the paragraph. Does it indicate the comparison or contrast pattern of writing? How? What might you change or add?

   _____

   _____

2. How many supporting sentences are in this paragraph? Write them down in the order they are discussed. How are they effective in explaining the topic sentence?

   _____

   _____

   _____

   _____

3. Circle the transition words. What order (time, space, or importance) is used to guide the reader from point to point? How effective are the transitions?

_____

_____

4. Underline all the development sentences (or FRIEDs); then, choose one of the development sentences from each supporting sentence in the paragraph, write it down, and state the kind of FRIED it is. Are there enough development sentences to explain each supporting idea?

_____

_____

_____

_____

5. State the concluding sentence. Identify the method (restating, observing, remarking, or summarizing) the writer uses to conclude the paragraph. Does the concluding sentence close off the paragraph or does it leave the reader hanging?

_____

_____

_____

6. State the point of view (first, second, or third person) used in this paragraph. Is it effective for the writer's purpose? Is it used consistently throughout?

_____

_____

7. What do you think of the title? Is it catchy? Is it reflective of what the paragraph discusses?

_____

_____

SUGGESTED TOPICS FOR WRITING COMPARISON OR CONTRAST PARAGRAPHS

Choose one of the following topics or use one of your own, and then use prewriting techniques to develop your draft for a comparison or contrast paragraph.

Any two fashion periods	Two previous jobs
Any two leaders	Two different coworkers
Any two social networking sites	Two different bosses
Any two careers	Any two methods of disciplining children
Any two sports	Your goals versus your reality
Any two bands	Any two YouTube presentations of a topic

▲ BUILDING SKILLS TOGETHER 7-2: Comparison or Contrast Paragraph Feedback Checklist

Once the rough draft for your comparison or contrast paragraph is completed, have a partner read it and answer the following revision and editing questions. You may also use this checklist to revise and edit your own paragraph.

Revising Paragraph Structure

☐ What is the topic sentence? What is the focused topic? How does the topic sentence indicate that comparison or contrast is the pattern used? What might you change or add?

☐ What similarities (or differences) are used as supporting sentences? How do they relate to the topic sentence? Are there enough sentences supporting the topic sentence? What might you change or add?

☐ Are clear transition words used to move you from one similarity (or difference) to another? Do they show an order of importance? What might you change or add?

☐ Are sufficient development sentences (or FRIEDs) used for each similarity (or difference) or supporting sentence? Where can you make improvements?

☐ How does the concluding sentence end the comparison/contrast paragraph? What concluding method (restating, observing, remarking, summarizing) is used?

☐ What point of view is used in the comparison or contrast paragraph? How relevant is it to the writer's purpose? Is it consistent throughout the paragraph? Are any changes needed?

☐ Is there a title? Is it catchy and reflective of the comparison or contrast paragraph?

Editing Spelling, Diction, and Sentence Construction

☐ Are there any misspelled words?

☐ Are appropriate and specific words used?

☐ Are any slang words, text message language, or clichés used?

☐ Consider the sentence structure and correct any errors with:

    ☐ Fragments, run-ons, and comma splices

    ☐ Misplaced or dangling modifiers

    ☐ Pronoun agreement

    ☐ Subject and verb agreement

Final Assessment

☐ What do you like the most about this paragraph?

☐ What are you unclear about or have difficulty with in this paragraph?

UNIT THREE: Building Loosely Structured Paragraphs

THE PARAGRAPHS PRESENTED in the following chapters do not follow a prescribed or formal structure when it comes to stating topic sentences, organizing supporting sentences, using development sentences, or presenting concluding sentences. For each of the following patterns, you will use different ways to create your topic sentence, to structure supporting and development sentences, and to conclude your paragraphs. The patterns of writing that lend themselves to informal structures are:

- Description
- Narration
- Definition

CHAPTER EIGHT: Description
Building Paragraphs with Imagery

Sometimes, you understand something better when someone describes it to you. For example, your doctor describes the flu symptoms you may experience, your friend describes the dream car he found at the car dealer, or your biology classmate describes the lab experiment you need to do. In many college classes, you are required to describe certain subjects.

Description creates a picture with words to help the reader see a person, place, object, or event. It selects details that build a sensory experience that *shows* rather than tells the topic. The purpose is to make the readers feel as if they are in that room with you or facing that person or holding that object. With the use of detailed worded imagery, you are able to bring a person, place, or object to life for the reader.

WRITING A DESCRIPTION PARAGRAPH

The main thrust of description is the impression you are trying to convey to the reader. The main impression or **dominant impression** is the overall sense, image, or effect you want to create for the reader through sensory details or the five senses. To write a descriptive paragraph:

1. Focus on a topic: a place, person, object, or event.
2. Engage the five senses—sight, sound, taste, smell, and touch—and prewrite ideas or images that come to mind about your topic. Use **objective** (factual) and **subjective** (personal reactions) description.
3. Look at the ideas in your prewriting and join those that seem to go together; then, see what overall mood they convey to you. That mood will be your dominant impression.

4. Decide what sensory details you will keep and what order of organization you will use to start your description. You might use **spatial** or **space order** in describing a person, place, or object, but you might use **time order** in describing an event.

5. Start writing a draft, being careful to use order and as much detailed sensory images as you can to support your dominant impression. Consider this list for generic sensory details.

Sight	colors
	shapes
	sizes
	patterns
	brightness
Sound	loud/soft
	piercing/soothing
Smell	sweet/sour
	sharp/mild
	cloying
	pungent
Taste	bitter
	sugary
	metallic
	spicy
Touch	hard/soft
	delicate/rough
	dry/oily
	smooth
	silky

6. Consider using similes and metaphors. Similes and metaphors both call attention to how two different things are similar. These powerful descriptive tools help you make a familiar thing look, sound, feel or behave like something else. They enable you to draw parallels between topics to clarify concepts for the reader and to conjure up images that are more instantly descriptive than a long section of writing.

A **simile** helps readers picture one thing as like another thing. A simile uses explicit comparison words such as *like* or *as*.

Simile: **Life is like a highway.**

On the other hand, a **metaphor** does not use direct comparison words. The metaphor goes a step further than the simile and instead of asking readers to picture one thing as being like another, readers picture one thing as being another.

Metaphor: **Life is a highway.**

 MEMORY TIP

There are no rules about when you should use a simile versus a metaphor. It depends on the effect you are trying to achieve. You can remember the difference between similes and metaphors by remembering that a simile has the letter *I* in it, just like the word *like*, which you use in a simile.

GENERIC PLAN FOR A DESCRIPTIVE PARAGRAPH

Note that although there is no set structure for descriptive writing, here is a generic plan of what a descriptive paragraph might look like.

Topic Sentence = Focused Topic (Topic + Dominant Impression)

First sensory image (sight)—details
Another sensory image (touch)—details
Another sensory image (smell)—details
Even more sensory image (hear)—details
Last sensory image (taste)—details

> Note: These sensory images can be moved around and can be put in any order that best fits your description.

Concluding Sentence

Consider a bedroom as a topic for a descriptive paragraph. Prewrite by listing sensory details or details for sight, smell, sound, taste, and touch. Here is a prewriting list:

sight: queen-sized mahogany bed, soft, aquamarine-blue walls, colorful and flowery bedspread, flower arrangement, tall mahogany dresser, cluttered working desk with a tall lamp, black iPod sound station, strewn shoes, posters of idols, television, computer, books, dog's bed in corner

touch: the soft, fuzzy bedspread, crisp linens

smell: vanilla-scented air from the candle, musty smell of worn shoes, socks, and sleep

> hear: brush of the palm tree limbs against the window pane, soothing classical music from iPod, serenity, soft-spinning hum of the ceiling fan blades
>
> taste: nothing applies

Topic Sentence

Your topic sentence in a descriptive paragraph contains the opinion or focused topic, which consists of the topic (person, place, object, or event) and the dominant impression. Generally, the dominant impression is one or two words that show the overall sense you want to leave with the reader about your topic.

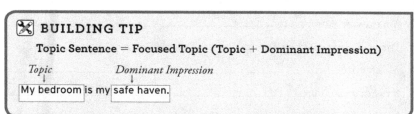

⚒ BUILDING TIP

Topic Sentence = Focused Topic (Topic + Dominant Impression)

Topic   *Dominant Impression*

My bedroom is my safe haven.

COMMON WORDS FOR DOMINANT IMPRESSIONS

Dominant impressions for places

crowded	inviting	drab	inspiring
tasteless	cheerful	gaudy	cozy
depressing	eerie	stuffy	dark
dazzling	restful	haunting	refuge

Dominant impressions for people

creative	angry	proud	generous
tense	silent	dependable	responsible
snobbish	shy	aggressive	witty

Dominant impressions for objects

sleek	rough	refreshing	lethal
weighty	spongy	velvety	delicate

Vague words to avoid		
good	bad	fun
nice	fine	beautiful
okay	normal	typical

BUILDING SKILLS 8-1: Creating Dominant Impressions

State a dominant impression—one or two words—to describe each of the following phrases. You may refer to the dominant impressions listed on pages 113–114.

1. The room you are now in: _____

2. A hardware store: _____

3. The home of your best friend: _____

4. A librarian: _____

5. A history teacher: _____

6. A soldier: _____

7. An old woman in a nursing home: _____

8. A drink of lemonade: _____

9. A refrigerator: _____

10. Fresh-baked bread: _____

11. A mousetrap: _____

Supporting and Development Sentences

In description, the supporting and development sentences merge, and they consist of the specific sensory details—touch, smell, taste, hearing, or sight—that specifically show the focused topic and dominant impression about a person, place, event, or object. The more details you use, the better your description. Be sure to use interesting descriptive vocabulary and stay away from overused words such as *good, bad, nice,* or *mean.* Most importantly, be sure to order your supporting sentences in a spatial (top to bottom, right to left, or outside to inside) or time (first to last) order, so the reader can move through your description with ease. Rely heavily on transitions. If you are describing a house, you may want to describe the outside of the house and then the inside, but do not shift the details back and forth as that confuses the reader. If you are describing a person, you might want to describe the face and head and then the body. A meal can be described from the first course to the last one. In the example of the bedroom, the supporting and development sentences would be all the sensory details listed in the brainstorm, but organized to show the bedroom in a logical manner.

> ### 🔧 BUILDING TIP
>
> Since you are usually writing about your own perspective and experience in a descriptive paragraph, most descriptive paragraphs require the use of **first-person point of view**, using the pronouns *I* or *we*.

BUILDING SKILLS 8-2: Finding Details for Support

Write three sensory details to support the dominant impression of each topic.

1. A fun party you attended

   _____

   _____

   _____

   _____

2. My messy office space

   _____

   _____

   _____

   _____

3. The bustling cafeteria at lunchtime

   _____

   _____

   _____

   _____

4. A sunrise at the beach

   _____

   _____

   _____

   _____

5. Your dream house

_____

_____

_____

_____

_____

BUILDING SKILLS 8-3: Identifying Sensory Details

Read this paragraph and identify the details that go with each of the senses then write down the dominant impression.

Kerosene stoves, with small black handles, were placed about to warm the shivering crowd. They stood around the blazing fire rubbing their hands and watching their clothes steam. Around them, the night blanketed the trees, and the misty rain fell softly. An old lady, in a slicker and rubber boots up to her knees, kept bringing bowls of spicy soup and shiny tin cups of steaming, nutty coffee.

Sight: _____

_____

Sound: _____

_____

Touch: _____

_____

Taste: _____

_____

Smell: _____

_____

Dominant Impression: _____

_____

> ## TRANSITIONS USED IN DESCRIPTION PARAGRAPHS
>
> Transitions are essential to a descriptive paragraph because they show the organization of your details. Be sure to use them so that you move the reader logically through your details.
>
> **Order of space**
>
> | from the top | to the left/right | to the back | in the corner | under | behind | next to | over |
> |---|---|---|---|---|---|---|---|
> | at the bottom | in the center | at the front | underneath | above | beside | outside | inside |
>
> **Order of time**
>
> | in the beginning | after | before | next | soon | while | then | last | finally |
> |---|---|---|---|---|---|---|---|---|
>
> Consult Appendix B for a complete list of transitions.

BUILDING SKILLS 8-4: Putting Details in Order

The details under each topic sentence are not in order. Put them in the right order by labeling them with numbers 1, 2, and so on.

1. Topic Sentence: The top drawer of my office desk is a mess.

   Details: _____ The cord I was looking for is all the way in the back.

   _____ Pencils, paperclips, and assorted change are scattered in the tray at the front of the drawer.

   _____ Some of the items near the back of the drawer are an empty tape dispenser, unfolded gum wrappers, and a stale candy bar.

   _____ Near the front of the drawer sit a crumpled, yellow sheet with a long number written on it, gas receipts, and a bank statement.

   _____ The first thing I see when I open the drawer is a jumble of papers.

2. Topic Sentence: The old cabin had an air of being lovingly cared for.

   Details: _____ The comfortable soft green sofas looked inviting in the main room.

   _____ The wood floors smelled of lemon pine.

   _____ Every tree leaned protectively over the cabin.

   _____ The front door had a welcome sign carved in it.

_____ The warmth from the roaring fire hugged the corners of the small cabin.

_____ The log cabin gleamed invitingly in the afternoon sun.

3. Topic Sentence: Business women are distinguishable by their good taste in dress.

Details: _____ Their skirts are handsomely cut.

_____ Shoes are sensible but beautiful.

_____ Their blouses and sweaters fit perfectly.

_____ They pay meticulous attention to their hairstyles and makeup.

_____ Around their necks are exquisite silk scarves.

4. Topic Sentence: My grandma's kitchen is a very warm and cheerful place.

Details: _____ To the back of the room, white porcelain dishes beckon me to come enjoy my grandmother's cherry pie.

_____ To my left, a big white refrigerator hums soothingly.

_____ By the door where I stand, the sun shines on the gleaming pine table.

_____ Looking across the room, I see the vase with fresh roses on the yellow-tiled countertop by the sink.

Concluding Sentence

The concluding sentence in a descriptive paragraph reminds the reader of the focused topic or the dominant impression about the person, place, object, or event and makes a final observation about the focused topic.

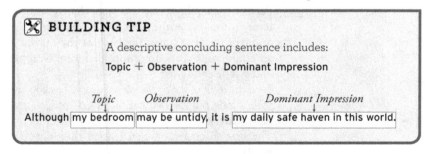

> ⚒ **BUILDING TIP**
>
> A descriptive concluding sentence includes:
>
> **Topic + Observation + Dominant Impression**
>
> *Topic*   *Observation*   *Dominant Impression*
>
> Although my bedroom may be untidy, it is my daily safe haven in this world.

EXAMPLE OF A DESCRIPTIVE PARAGRAPH

Topic: my bedroom

My Safe Haven

At the end of every day, I come to my safe haven: my bedroom. My bedroom walls are a soft, aquamarine-blue color. In the middle of the room is the queen-sized mahogany bed with the colorful, tropical-flowered bedspread covers and crisp blue linens. My bedspread is soft and fuzzy to the touch, but it hugs my favorite place in the world, my bed. To the left of the bed is my tall, sturdy mahogany dresser that houses six draw-ers filled with my colorful, fashionable clothes. Next to that is my clut-tered working desk with a tall lamp, my computer, and my black iPod sound station. Directly across from my bed and mounted on the wall is the 24-inch flat-screen television surrounded by seven colorful posters of my favorite bands and idols. To the right of my bed and over by the bedroom door sits my dog's brown, fluffy fleece bed. Strewn all over the bedroom's cherry-colored hardwood floors are worn shoes and socks, piles of dirty laundry, and scattered textbooks. Thankfully, the vanilla-scented candle cleverly masks the dirty laundry smell. The brush of the palm tree limbs against the windowpane creates a calming sound that accompanies the soft music coming from my iPod and if I listen carefully, I hear the soft-spinning hum of the ceiling fan blades. The sounds in my room are the sounds of serenity and peace, and the mood in my room is one of freedom and security and that is why my room is my safe haven in this world.

BUILDING SKILLS TOGETHER 8-1: Evaluating Description Paragraphs

Working in a small group, read the following paragraphs and answer the evalua-tion questions that follow.

A Place

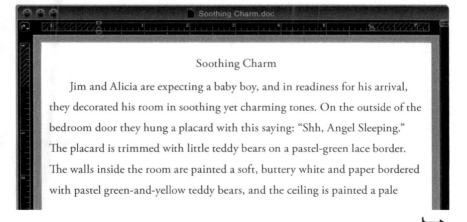

Soothing Charm

Jim and Alicia are expecting a baby boy, and in readiness for his arrival, they decorated his room in soothing yet charming tones. On the outside of the bedroom door they hung a placard with this saying: "Shh, Angel Sleeping." The placard is trimmed with little teddy bears on a pastel-green lace border. The walls inside the room are painted a soft, buttery white and paper bordered with pastel green-and-yellow teddy bears, and the ceiling is painted a pale green. Past the white doorway and to the right sits the rectangular crib. The crib is made of white wood furnished with white, pastel green, and Easter yellow linens. A mobile with soft, cloth bears dangles and dances over the crib. To the left of the crib a white wooden rocking chair with striped pale green cushions beckons the visitors. A big, white wooden toy chest sits patiently in the corner of the room. To the left of the entryway stands a tall, four-drawer dresser made of white wood trimmed with green handles. Undoubtedly, Jim and Alicia's baby boy will spend many soothing hours in his charming room.

A Person

Glamorous Model.doc

Glamorous Model

My eighteen-year-old sister looks like a glamorously dressed model. Her thick, long, curly black hair gleams with coconut-smelling mousse. Her heart-shaped face frames a pair of sparkling, almond-shaped dark chocolate eyes, a pointed, straight small nose, and pouting, full cherry-colored lips. Her dark-brown complexion makes her high cheekbones glow with a healthy tint. Around her stout neck is a shimmering red scarf that falls onto a blouse of silver sequins. Her blouse rests comfortably on her plump, rounded shoulders and exposes her chubby, brown arms. The short, red leather skirt hugs her voluptuous waist and shows off her shapely, thick legs. Around her right ankle sparkles a platinum bracelet. The heels on her embellished silver sandals are three inches high, and they flatter her large, well-proportioned feet and display her bright, cherry-lacquered toenails. My dark-skinned sister is attractive, but when she is glamorously dressed, she looks like a stylish model.

An Object

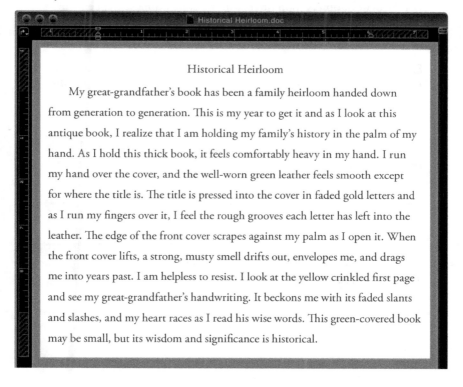

Historical Heirloom

My great-grandfather's book has been a family heirloom handed down from generation to generation. This is my year to get it and as I look at this antique book, I realize that I am holding my family's history in the palm of my hand. As I hold this thick book, it feels comfortably heavy in my hand. I run my hand over the cover, and the well-worn green leather feels smooth except for where the title is. The title is pressed into the cover in faded gold letters and as I run my fingers over it, I feel the rough grooves each letter has left into the leather. The edge of the front cover scrapes against my palm as I open it. When the front cover lifts, a strong, musty smell drifts out, envelopes me, and drags me into years past. I am helpless to resist. I look at the yellow crinkled first page and see my great-grandfather's handwriting. It beckons me with its faded slants and slashes, and my heart races as I read his wise words. This green-covered book may be small, but its wisdom and significance is historical.

For each paragraph, answer the following questions:

1. Underline the topic sentence. What does the writer state as the topic and the dominant impression?

   _____

   _____

2. Are the sensory details sufficient to show the dominant impression? What could be improved?

   _____

   _____

3. Circle the transitions. How effective are the transitions at moving you through the paragraph? What changes might you make?

   _____

   _____

4. Underline the concluding sentence. Is the dominant impression restated and is a thoughtful observation offered in the concluding sentence?

_____

_____

5. State the point of view (first, second, or third person) used in this paragraph. Is it effective for the writer's purpose? Is it used consistently throughout?

_____

_____

6. What do you think of the title? Is it catchy? Is it reflective of what the paragraph discusses?

_____

_____

SUGGESTED TOPICS FOR WRITING DESCRIPTION PARAGRAPHS

Choose one of the following topics or use one of your own, and then use prewriting techniques to develop your draft for a description paragraph.

A favorite place
A favorite photograph or piece of clothing
An uncomfortable room
An event with joyful celebrations
An object such as a cell phone, key chain, bracelet, ring, or necklace
Your own space at work
A coworker or relative
A product or service you sell or make at your workplace

 BUILDING SKILLS TOGETHER 8-2: Description
Paragraph Feedback Checklist

Once the rough draft of your description paragraph is completed, have a partner read it and answer the following revision and editing questions. You may also use this checklist to revise and edit your own paragraph.

Revising Paragraph Structure

☐ What is the topic sentence? What topic is being described? What dominant impression is given about the topic? What might you change?

☐ Are there sufficient descriptive sensory details to support, develop, or show the focused topic—the dominant impression about the person, place, object, or event? What could be improved?

☐ Are there clear transition words that move you from one sensory detail to another? In what order (spatial or time) are the descriptive details organized? What might you change or add?

☐ Does the concluding sentence remind the reader of the dominant impression and make a final or thoughtful observation about the topic?

☐ What point of view is used in this descriptive paragraph? How relevant is it to the writer's purpose? Is it consistent throughout the paragraph? Are any changes needed?

☐ Is there a title? Is it catchy and reflective of the description paragraph?

Editing Spelling, Diction, and Sentence Construction

☐ Are there misspelled words?

☐ Are appropriate and specific words used?

☐ Are slang words, text message language, or clichés used?

☐ Consider the sentence structure and correct any errors with:

   ☐ Fragments, run-ons, and comma splices

   ☐ Misplaced or dangling modifiers

   ☐ Pronoun agreement

   ☐ Subject and verb agreement

Final Assessment

☐ What do you like the most about this paragraph?

☐ What are you unclear about or have difficulty with in this paragraph?

CHAPTER NINE: Narration
Building Paragraphs with Stories

In television shows, in novels and fairy tales, or in social gatherings, you are entertained by scary, funny, or silly stories. Although you connect with others through that medium, you also use it to share your experiences and your knowledge. In some college classes, you are required to tell stories about a number of subjects from perseverance in facing obstacles to heartbreak or historical tragedies.

A narrative paragraph is often a storytelling paragraph designed to share experiences or life lessons. Real or made-up stories can entertain, instruct, clarify, or persuade readers and help them understand and cope with the world. When you write a real or made-up narrative, you focus on a particular experience or situation and make a specific point about it to make it significant for the readers to understand something about themselves, about other people, or about the world they live in.

Stories may be told using the **past tense** because they may be experiences that have happened in the past to you or to others. Usually, stories have endings, and these endings signal that the narratives have happened in the past. As you become more skillful at writing narratives, you may venture beyond the past tense, but for now, writing stories using the past tense is a good place to start. You can tell stories in one of two points of view:

- **First-person narration:** This is when you describe a personal experience using first-person pronouns such as *I* or *we*.
- **Third-person narration**: This is when you describe what happened to someone else, and you use third-person pronouns such as *he, she,* or *they.*

MEMORY TIP

Point of view identifies from whose perspective the story is told. There are three kinds of points of view, but generally the first- and third-person points of view are most commonly used in narratives.

- **First-person** point of view uses the pronouns *I* or *we*. In a first-person narrative, the story is conveyed by a narrator who is also a character within the story. It is used as a way to communicate the internal or unspoken thoughts of the narrator.

- **Second-person** point of view uses the pronouns *you* or *your*. It is the rarest mode in literature or storytelling because the narrator refers to one of the characters as *you*, therefore making the audience member feel as if he or she is a character within the story.

- **Third-person** point of view uses the pronouns *she, he, it, they, him, her,* or names of people. Third-person narration provides the greatest flexibility to the author and thus is the most commonly used narrative mode in literature. In a third-person narrative, the narrator does not participate in the action of the story as one of the characters, but lets readers know exactly how the characters feel. You learn about the characters through this outside voice.

Refer to Chapter One for a complete explanation of point of view.

WRITING A NARRATION PARAGRAPH

To write a narrative paragraph, decide on the experience or situation you want to focus on showing and the lesson you want to share with the reader. Sometimes you may not have a clear idea of the lesson you want to share, but write the draft anyway and along the way the lesson will become clearer. At other times you may know what lesson you want to share, but you may not have an actual story. You can make one up, but whether you make it up or it is real, a good way to learn strong narrative skills is by learning and mastering five elements.

- **B**ackground
- **C**onflict
- **O**rder of events
- **O**utcome
- **L**esson

These elements make it easier for the writer to build a story with a good beginning, middle, and ending.

> ### 👆 MEMORY TIP
>
> The five elements in a narrative make up the acronym BCOOL (pronounced as *be cool*):
>
> - **B**ackground
> - **C**onflict
> - **O**rder of events
> - **O**utcome
> - **L**esson
>
> Although BCOOL is not the only way to tell a story, it is one effective way that makes it easier to write a narrative. As you get more practice, you can begin to experiment by putting these elements in different orders, or using only some of the elements.

Using a made-up scenario involving heartache as the topic, look at how these elements help create a narrative:

1. **B**ackground: This should appear in several sentences after your topic sentence. This specifies where and when the situation happened and who was or were involved. It is the description of the situation's time, location, and people, and may be described briefly or at length.

> Hottest day in August at a Macy's Mall; fragrance and cosmetic counter. Paul and unknown girl—twenty feet apart. Paul liked the girl but had never talked to her.

2. **C**onflict: This is the heart of the narrative. It is what the narrative tries to solve. It shows what the problem is. The problem could be one of the following:
   - man vs. man: a person against another person or a group of people
   - man vs. nature: a person or persons against a force of nature like a blizzard, tornado, starvation
   - man vs. himself: a person against an internal fear or insecurity like a fear of heights or commitment

> man vs. man: He wanted to talk to her, get to know her before he quit his job for the summer.

3. **O**rder of events: This is the step-by-step sequence of events to show how the conflict is being dealt with. This is the longest and most descriptive part of the narrative. Here is where the details have to be vivid and well-organized, the suspense is built, and dialogue is used.

> First, Paul decided to approach on that day right before closing time.
> Then, Paul picked up a woman's perfume bottle and crossed to her cosmetic counter.
> Next, Paul quickly blurted: "Hi, I'm trying to buy a birthday gift for my Mom, and I wonder if you'd tell me if this is an appropriate fragrance for her?"
> Finally, Paul had a conversation with her and found out that she is leaving her job at the end of the week.

4. **O**utcome: This is the result of the conflict: the solution. This may be briefly stated in a few sentences.

> She has a boyfriend, and she is moving to Atlanta with him.

5. **Le**sson: This answers the "so what" question for the reader. It is the importance of the story; the lesson learned, realized, shown, or shared with the reader. It can be simply stated or implied. It can appear in the topic sentence and be implied or restated in the concluding sentence.

> Heartache hurts but especially when what we desire is unattainable.

 BUILDING TIP

1. The use of **description** (imagery of the characters, the places, the objects in the story) and **transitions** (words that help the reader move from idea to idea) are not only required for narrative paragraphs but also mandatory to enhance and enrich your narrative.

2. Sometimes, **dialogue** is used to show the interactions between the story's characters. Dialogue shows the conversations or verbal exchanges between characters. Dialogue must be put inside quotations marks (" ") and must follow a conversational tag word such as *said, exclaimed, cried*. Commas follow the conversational tag word and periods at the end of statements must go inside the second quotation mark.

   Ron turned to Sara and said, "I am glad you joined us on this hike."

   Sara replied, "Something told me I should not miss this adventure."

After you have broken down your story into the five elements, you can write it as a paragraph. In your paragraph, do not announce the BCOOL elements like this:

The conflict was ...

The order of events is seen ...

In other words, do not tell the reader your story, but show or reveal your story. To show your story, organize your thoughts based on the BCOOL elements but express them in engaging language that describes the background, conflict, order of events, and outcome.

GENERIC PLAN FOR A NARRATIVE PARAGRAPH

Topic Sentence = Focused Topic (Experience + Lesson)
Background information sentences
Conflict description sentences
Order of events sentences
    First event—details
    Second event—details
    Third event—details
    Fourth event—details
Outcome sentences
Concluding sentence or lesson

Topic Sentence

A narrative may make a point about an experience so that the reader is interested in reading it. For example, a story about just finding a wallet is not as interesting as a story about having your honesty tested after finding a wallet.

The topic sentence should include your opinion about a given experience, which is the focused topic of your story. In other words, the topic sentence for a narrative may be a general statement about an experience and the lesson learned or realized from it. The lesson is the meaning the reader may take from your experience; it is the answer to the "so what?" question about your story. To create a meaningful topic sentence, ask yourself these questions: How did I (or the main character) change? What did I (or the main character) learn? What is important to me (or to the main character) about this experience?

Wrong: I skydive.
Right: A skydiving experience showed me how precious life is.

> ### 🛠 BUILDING TIP
>
> **Topic Sentence = Focused Topic (Experience + Lesson Learned)**
>
> *Experience*   *Lesson Learned*
>
> An experience with a cosmetic girl | taught Paul the meaning of heartache.

BUILDING SKILLS 9-1: Deciding on a Lesson

Write a main point or lesson for each topic.

1. Topic: A fight I had with my best friend.
   Lesson: _____
   _____

2. Topic: A frightening experience at work or school.
   Lesson: _____
   _____

BUILDING SKILLS 9-2: Recognizing Effective Narration Topic Sentences

Put a check mark next to the topic sentences that are effective narrative topic sentences.

_____ 1. Acts of kindness will be the subject of this paragraph.

_____ 2. A friend's betrayal tested my sense of loyalty.

_____ 3. Two dogs are lost on our street.

_____ 4. Winning the swimming competition increased my sister's self-confidence and self-worth.

_____ 5. Someone took my laptop computer.

_____ 6. This is a paragraph about two brothers fighting.

_____ 7. I want to tell you about my first time selling hot dogs.

_____ 8. The snake found in my bed will be discussed.

_____ 9. Loving someone has taught me the value of sacrifice.

_____ 10. My last drink of alcohol was the beginning of a better life through better health.

BUILDING SKILLS 9-3: Completing the BCOOL Pattern

1. Topic: A frightening situation
   Background: An elevator in a high-rise building malfunctions and gets stuck between two floors.
   Conflict: Person stuck inside has claustrophobia or fear of tight spaces.

   Order of Events: _____

   _____

   _____

   Outcome: _____

   _____

   _____

   Lesson: _____

   _____

   _____

2. Topic: Money theft
   Background: An employee at a coffee house stole money from the register.
   Conflict: The other employees do not know what to do.

   Order of Events: _____

   _____

   _____

   Outcome: _____

   _____

   _____

   Lesson: _____

   _____

   _____

Supporting and Development Sentences

The support for the topic sentence comes from the list of major events in the story and their detailed explanations. The unfolding of events should include the BCOOL elements and build to a climax or peak before the conflict is resolved.

Be selective in which events you include because you want to have the ones that most clearly demonstrate your lesson.

The development sentences in narratives come from the vivid details you use to show the story. These details add interest and suspense to the story and involve readers. Refer to Chapter Nine for help with sensory details. Be sure to use vivid details and dialogue to enrich your narrative.

In narrative paragraphs, support and development sentences go hand in hand with transitions, especially time or chronological transitions, because they make the order of events clearer to readers. In the heartache example, the supporting and development sentences describe the conflict, order of events, and the outcome.

TRANSITIONS USED IN NARRATION PARAGRAPHS

after	eventually	meanwhile	soon	earlier
as	finally	next	then	suddenly
at last	first	now	when	by this time
before	. last	second	while	as soon as
during	later	since		

Phrases with specific times or dates such as *in 2001... after two days...at 2 o'clock...two minutes later...*

Consult Appendix B for a complete list of transitions.

BUILDING SKILLS 9-4: Identifying Support

Read the following paragraph, and under each appropriate heading that follows, list the supporting details that fit each narrative element.

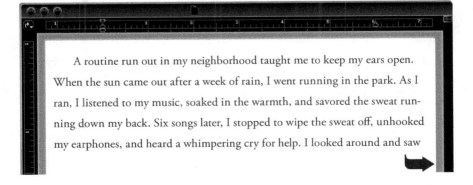

A routine run out in my neighborhood taught me to keep my ears open. When the sun came out after a week of rain, I went running in the park. As I ran, I listened to my music, soaked in the warmth, and savored the sweat running down my back. Six songs later, I stopped to wipe the sweat off, unhooked my earphones, and heard a whimpering cry for help. I looked around and saw a small male child hanging upside down in the middle of the monkey bars. It appeared that he had miscalculated his reach and got himself stuck upside down with his legs stuck behind him. He must have been hanging there for a while because his face was red from the blood rushing to it. I ran to him and started to disengage his stuck legs. I grabbed him by the shoulders, pried him off the monkey bars, and set him down on the grass. He moaned with pain as the blood rushed to his extremities. Then, he turned to me and softly and slowly said, "Thank you for helping me. I have been calling for help for forever and I was scared no one would come." I stayed with him for a while longer, and we talked about many things. Two hours later, I learned that he is eight years old, and he lives ten houses down from mine. After I walked him home and met his wonderful family, I decided I would no longer wear earphones when I run, so I can keep my ears and eyes open at all times.

From this narrative, list details about the:

Background: _____

_____

_____

_____

_____

Conflict: _____

_____

_____

_____

_____

Order of events: _____

_____

_____

_____

_____

Outcome: _____

_____

_____

_____

_____

Lesson: _____
_____
_____
_____
_____

Concluding Sentence

The concluding sentence in a narrative restates the topic sentence and offers a thoughtful remark about the experience or lesson. Avoid announcing the lesson; instead, state it clearly as part of a sentence that highlights the experience.

> **BUILDING TIP**
>
> A narrative concluding sentence includes: **Lesson + Experience**
>
> *Lesson*   *Experience*
>   ↓   ↓
> | Paul learned the meaning of heartache | after | talking to the girl he liked. |

EXAMPLE OF A NARRATION PARAGRAPH

Topic: heartache

Cosmetic Girl

Yesterday, on the hottest day in August, Paul learned what heartache feels like. He worked part-time at the Macy's fragrance counter, and she worked at the cosmetics counter twenty feet away. They had never talked. He did not know her name, but Paul thought she was the most beautiful girl he had ever seen. In two days, his summer vacation would end, and he would quit his job to start a new semester in college. Running out of time and desperate, Paul approached her one day fifteen minutes before closing time. He crossed the twenty feet that separated them. She smiled at him as he approached, and he cleared his throat, lifted a perfume bottle, and quickly blurted, "Hi, I am trying to buy a birthday gift for my Mom, and I wonder if you'd tell me if this is an appropriate fragrance for her?" Delicately, she sniffed at the perfume and declared that his mother would love it. Empowered to carry on a conversation with her, Paul asked about her plans for the rest of summer, and that was when she told him she was leaving at the end of the week because she and her boyfriend of three years were moving to Atlanta next week. Numbly, Paul averted his eyes to hide his pain, thanked her for her help, and went back to his counter. The twenty feet of space became a crushing heartache. Although he still did not know her name, Paul had two wretched days of work still to go.

BUILDING SKILLS TOGETHER 9-1: Evaluating a Narration Paragraph

Working in a small group, read the following paragraph and answer the evaluation questions that follow.

Terror at the Beach

My idyllic day at the beach ended in terror that taught me the importance of vigilance. My family and I went to Huntington Beach State Park for one of our family reunions. At the beach, we played volleyball and built sand castles until the sun set. Then, we made room for the bonfire and the s'mores. While I packed, I overheard Brianna, my six-year-old niece, ask my mother if she could get a roasting stick that she had found by the palm trees. My mother agreed, and Brianna dashed off. An hour later, my sister-in-law screamed, "Brianna is missing!" Suddenly, everyone got up and started walking in different directions calling Brianna's name. Panic set in my legs and heart, and I started out toward the public restrooms. As I approached, I heard a sniffle. I aimed my flashlight at where I thought the sniffle came from and saw Brianna's tear-stained face. I ran to her and hugged her laughing and crying. After I got her back into her parents' arms, we were all relieved that she was safe. As our adrenaline rush simmered down, we decided that children are not allowed to wander alone from now on; they must be accompanied by an adult at all times. Although Brianna was gone for only an hour, it felt like a lifetime, a feeling I never want to feel again. The day my niece went missing was the day I truly learned terror and appreciated how important vigilance is with children.

1. Underline the topic sentence. What experience and lesson are indicated in the topic sentence? State the focused topic.

   _____

   _____

2. What details describe the background?

   _____

   _____

3. What details describe the conflict?

   _____

   _____

4. What details describe the order of events?

   _____

   _____

5. What details describe the outcome?

   _____

   _____

6. Underline the concluding sentence. How does it conclude the narrative? What is the lesson? What is the experience?

   _____

   _____

7. State the point of view (first, second, or third person) used in this paragraph. Is it effective for the writer's purpose? Is it used consistently throughout?

   _____

   _____

8. What do you think of the title? Is it catchy? Is it reflective of what the paragraph discusses?

   _____

   _____

SUGGESTED TOPICS FOR WRITING NARRATION PARAGRAPHS

Choose one of the following topics or use one of your own, and then use prewriting techniques to develop a draft for a narration paragraph.

A scandal
A good or bad decision
Accepting a dare that led to trouble
A dangerous situation
An instance of injustice
Unexpected good luck
A disagreement with a family member
A bullying situation
An ethical dilemma at work
A customer-service disagreement
Pick a saying as the lesson of your narrative:
Better to be alone than in bad company
Nice people finish last
It isn't what you know; it's who you know
Honey catches more flies than vinegar
If you can't beat them, join them
All that glitters is not gold

 BUILDING SKILLS TOGETHER 9-2: Narration Paragraph Feedback Checklist

Once the rough draft of your narration paragraph is complete, have a partner read it and answer the following revision and editing questions. You may also use this checklist to revise and edit your own paragraph.

Revising Paragraph Structure

☐ Does the topic sentence indicate the focused topic of a lesson learned from an experience, situation, or event? If not, what might you change?

☐ Does the writer use the BCOOL pattern to support the topic sentence? Are there enough sentences supporting the topic sentence? What might you change or add?

☐ Underline the sentences that describe the background. Are there enough details about the background? What changes can you make or add?

☐ Double-underline the sentences that present the conflict. What changes can you make or add?

☐ Bracket the sentences that present the order of events. What changes can you make or add?

☐ Highlight the sentences that provide the outcome. Was the result an effective solution to the conflict? How so?

☐ Circle the sentences that provide the meaning or lesson to the narrative. Do you think the meaning or significance of this narrative is strong and relevant? What changes can you make or add?

☐ Are there clear transition words to move you through the order of events? What might you change or add?

☐ Does the concluding sentence close with a thoughtful remark and remind the reader of the experience and lesson?

☐ What point of view is used in the narrative? How relevant is it to the writer's purpose? Is it consistent throughout the paragraph? Are any changes needed?

☐ Is there a title? Is it catchy and reflective of the narration paragraph?

Editing Spelling, Diction, and Sentence Construction

☐ Are there any misspelled words?

☐ Are appropriate and specific words used?

☐ Are slang words, text message language, or clichés used?

☐ Consider the sentence structure and correct any errors with:

    ☐ Fragments, run-ons, and comma splices

    ☐ Misplaced or dangling modifiers

    ☐ Pronoun agreement

    ☐ Subject and verb agreement

Final Assessment

☐ What do you like the most about this paragraph?

☐ What are you unclear about or have difficulty with in this paragraph?

CHAPTER TEN: Definition
Building Paragraphs with Clarifications

You might say that your friend has *charm* or that your car shows *prestige*. Without some explanation, these italicized terms mean very little. To make your meaning clear, you could define what you mean. Some college assignments may involve the use of definitions; for example, in a biology paper, you may be asked to define meiosis; in an economics paper, you may be asked to define inflation; in a history paper, you may be asked to define colonialism.

Definition is writing that explains what something means. The word *definition* leads many people to think of a dictionary, but defining involves more than looking up the meaning of a word. Defining involves two kinds of meaning or definitions: denotation and connotation.

Denotation is the actual meaning for a word—often found in a dictionary.

In the dictionary, the word *alien* is defined as "a being from another planet."

Connotation is the implied suggested meaning for a word—not necessarily found in a dictionary.

Connotations for the word *alien* include such notions as "strange, unfamiliar, or foreign."

In writing definition paragraphs, you may consult the dictionary for the meaning of a word—the denotation—but you write your paragraph about your own personal interpretation of the word—the connotation. You develop and show your own definition of the term—your own connotation.

WRITING A DEFINITION PARAGRAPH

When you write a definition paragraph, you need to understand the term you are using before you can define it for others. Start by reading the dictionary's definition of your term and prewriting ideas about its meaning. Then, explain the term in your own words. A good strategy to follow in your definition paragraph is:

1. Decide on the term you want to define.
2. Develop your own personal definition for it using one of the following ways:
   - **Definition by synonym:** Use a word that means the same thing as your term.
     Success means achievement.
   - **Definition by negation:** Explain what the term is not.
     Success is not the amount of money one has.
   - **Definition by category:** Defining by category has two parts: the general category the word belongs to and the way the word is distinguished or distinctive from other words in that group. For example, heart is in the category of organ, but it is different from other organs like brain, lungs, liver, and so on, because it pumps blood. Consider this example:

A dictator is a leader who has absolute power over his subjects.
Term   Category   Distinction

3. Decide how you will organize your explanation of the definition. Here is where you draw on any of the other writing patterns (illustration, cause or effect, comparison or contrast, narration or description) to develop your explanations.

✂ BUILDING TIP

Definition paragraphs do not follow any one specific pattern of development; instead, they use any or a mix of the writing patterns discussed in previous chapters. Often, description paragraphs use a combination of patterns; for example, a definition paragraph may define the term *success* and discuss it by giving examples and narrating a story.

To decide on a pattern of organization, reflect on the best pattern or patterns that help you show or explain your term. You may want to refer to the previous chapters about the different writing patterns. Some patterns will be more useful for particular terms, so use the pattern that best suits your purpose.

Suppose you use the word *hero* for a working definition paragraph. According to Webster's *New World Dictionary,* the term *hero* means "any person admired for courage, nobility, or exploits especially in war. Any person admired for qualities or achievements and regarded as an ideal or model." You can define this term in three ways: by synonym, by negation, or by category. Approach the definition essay by identifying your connotative definition of the term and by deciding on the writing pattern to use in organizing your explanation of the definition. Once these steps are completed, you can start writing a rough draft.

GENERIC PLAN FOR A DEFINITION PARAGRAPH

Topic Sentence: focused topic (your definition of the term)

Supporting and Development Sentences: organized based on selected writing pattern or patterns

Concluding Sentence: restatement of definition and final observation

Topic Sentence

The topic sentence in a definition paragraph should show the focused topic, which is your own definition of the term and the pattern intended for development. Your definition is the way you view that term. You can state your definition in one of several ways: by synonym, by negation, or by category.

🔧 BUILDING TIP

Topic Sentence by Synonym = Term + means/is +definition

> **A hero is an idol.**

Topic Sentence by Negation = Term +is not + definition

> **A hero is not a loser.**

Topic Sentence by Category = Term + is+ category + definition

> **A hero is a person who has noble accomplishments.**

Whichever way you decide to state your definition, be sure to use the words *means* and *is* in your topic sentence and avoid troublesome constructions like *is when* or *is where.*

> ### 🛠 BUILDING TIP
>
> Avoid using the *is when* or *is where* expressions in your topic sentence because they limit your definition, implying that your term can only hold true in specific conditions.
>
> **Writer's block is when one is not able to start writing.**
>
> This topic sentence implies that whenever one is not able to start writing, one must have writer's block. So, what about those who are not able to start writing because they have yet to receive the assignment?

Supporting and Development Sentences

The supporting sentences in a definition paragraph are the examples, explanations, and facts that clarify your term. Their content and structure depends on the writing pattern you have selected to use. You may use illustration, description, cause and effect, comparison and contrast, and narration or a combination of a few to develop your definition paragraph. Some patterns or a combination of patterns will be more useful for particular terms. Use patterns that best suit your purpose. Refer back to the previous chapters about the different writing patterns. Here is a prewrite of some possible writing patterns for hero:

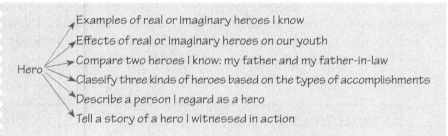

Which pattern seems most interesting to you? Pick that one and use it as the organizing pattern for your support and development. Consider illustration as a pattern for a *hero* paragraph.

> ### TRANSITIONS USED IN DEFINITION PARAGRAPHS
>
> The transitions you use in definition paragraphs depend on the pattern of writing you are using for support and development. Consult the individual chapters of the writing patterns or the complete guide to transitions in Appendix B.
>
> In keeping with the example of illustration as the organizing pattern for a hero paragraph, use the transitions that correspond with that writing pattern: first example, another example, and most important example.

Concluding Sentence
The concluding sentence ends the discussion by restating the definition of the term and by offering a final observation. For a concluding sentence about the example on hero, the final sentence could repeat the three or more examples in the order they were presented in the paragraph and end with a thoughtful restatement of the term's definition.

> My father, my uncle, and my niece are three amazing heroes or noble people who have accomplished so much in fighting to overcome their obstacles.

Another way to end the concluding sentence for the hero paragraph is simply to offer a general thoughtful observation about the term.

> Noble people who accomplish so much by overcoming their obstacles should be recognized as our real heroes.

EXAMPLE OF A DEFINITION PARAGRAPH
Topic: hero   Method of Organization: illustration

Noble Heroes

A hero is a person who has noble accomplishments, and I have the privilege of knowing several heroes who have made a significant impact on my life. My first hero is my father. My father grew up in a poor family with 11 siblings. He never got the chance to go to school or get an education, and at age thirteen, he started working construction to help feed his siblings. He spent his teen years toiling from sun up until sun down. At age nineteen, he started his own construction company and hired his previous coworkers as his workers. Thirty-six years later, he has a construction business empire and a college degree that has taken twelve years to finish. My second hero is my Uncle Tony. He was a firefighter and, on a daily basis, he put his life at risk to help others. He was married to his work, and he loved all the good and the bad that came with it. He gave up his eyesight and legs helping rescue a baby from a burning building; as a result, he had to relearn how to live life with severe limitations. He shows me what it means to be noble. My most impressive hero is Matilda, my eight-year-old niece. She is fighting a grave battle with brain cancer and yet she is always optimistic and cheerful. She is often in pain from blinding headaches and the side effects of chemotherapy, but she finds the time and effort to make those around her feel appreciated. Every day she shows me that no matter how bad life gets, there is always hope or a positive aspect somewhere. My father, my uncle, and my niece are three amazing heroes or noble people who have accomplished so much in fighting to overcome their obstacles.

✒ BUILDING SKILLS TOGETHER 10-1: Evaluating a Definition Paragraph

Working in a small group, read the following paragraphs and answer the evaluation questions that follow.

Paragraph 1
Topic: cheating in school

Offensive Learning.doc

Offensive Learning

Cheating in school is an offensive act that carries severe repercussions. One effect of cheating in school may be expulsion. In some academic institutions, cheating is a significant violation punishable by issuing a failing grade in the subject and by discharging the student from the institution. It is seen as an act of dishonesty and deception; as a result, the person who cheated may not be trusted again and therefore may be removed. It is believed that the threat of expulsion may be a deterrent for more cheating. Another effect may be documentation of the cheating offense in a student's permanent record or transcript, which follows him or her all through his or her academic life. All other schools will know about the offense and may deny admittance to that student. The gravest effect is that the student really could cheat him- or herself out of learning. The convenience of cheating creates in the student a false sense of success in a course that is essential for other courses. Therefore, the student who has cheated him or herself out of learning the necessary skills in the previous course may suffer during the subsequent course. That loss of learning may haunt that student as he or she progresses through school and at some point that student may end up having to relearn what was missed before. In the end, cheating in school may serve to deceive the student into thinking he has outsmarted the teacher and the school, but ultimately, that student may be deceiving and misleading himself or herself. Expulsion, permanent documentation, and lack of learning are some severe effects of deceiving the teacher by cheating in school.

1. Underline the topic sentence. How does it provide a focused topic? What definition does it show?

   _____

   _____

2. Is the term defined by synonym, by negation, or by category?

   _____

3. What pattern of writing (illustration, cause or effect, comparison or contrast, description, or narration) is used to support and develop the definition?

   _____

   _____

4. What transitions are used to move the reader through the paragraph? How effective are the transitions?

   _____

   _____

5. State the concluding sentence. Does the concluding sentence close off the paragraph or does it leave the reader hanging? Does it offer a final observation?

   _____

   _____

6. State the point of view (first, second, or third person) used in this paragraph. Is it effective for the writer's purpose? Is it used consistently throughout?

   _____

   _____

7. What do you think of the title? Is it catchy? Is it reflective of what the paragraph discusses?

   _____

   _____

Paragraph 2
Topic: money

Money Is Security

Some people see money as evil while others see it as something to spend on life's pleasures. My definition of money comes from my childhood experience where I learned that money means security. When I was growing up, my family was comfortable; my parents had good jobs, and I was always told that money was not important. Family, love, and home mattered most. Then, when I was fourteen, my father lost his job when his company downsized, and my mother started carrying the financial load for the family. In time, my parents' marriage became strained, and their fights grew louder and more aggressive, and it was harder for my brother and me to avoid hearing their arguments. Eventually they sat us down and told us that we could no longer keep the house we lived in because of the expensive monthly payment. We moved into my grandparents' house, and my father finally found a job. His job was three hundred miles away, so he moved out, but we stayed with my grandparents. My parents called it a "trial separation" at first; then, it became a "divorce." From the day he moved out, we never saw him again, and our family was broken. My brother and I felt cheated and betrayed; everything my parents had told us about money was a lie. They had said money was not important, but without it, the things that were important were gone. Now, I know that money is important and while it never can replace family, home, and love, it can keep them secure. For every family, big or small, money is security.

1. Underline the topic sentence. How does it provide a focused topic? What definition does it show?

_____

_____

2. Is the term defined by synonym, by negation, or by category?

_____

3. What pattern of writing (illustration, cause or effect, comparison or contrast, description, or narration) is used to support and develop the definition?

_____

_____

4. What transitions are used to move the reader through the paragraph? How effective are the transitions?

_____

_____

5. State the concluding sentence. Does the concluding sentence close off the paragraph or does it leave the reader hanging? Does it offer a final observation?

_____

_____

6. State the point of view (first, second, or third person) used in this paragraph. Is it effective for the writer's purpose? Is it used consistently throughout?

_____

_____

7. What do you think of the title? Is it catchy? Is it reflective of what the paragraph discusses?

_____

_____

_____

SUGGESTED TOPICS FOR WRITING DEFINITION PARAGRAPHS

Choose one of the following topics or use one of your own, and then use prewriting techniques to develop your draft for a definition paragraph.

Road rage	Self-respect
Arrogance	Customer service
Courage	Success
Democracy	Discrimination
Music	Greed
Celebrity	Identity

BUILDING SKILLS TOGETHER 10-2: Definition
Paragraph Feedback Checklist

Once the rough draft of your definition paragraph is completed, have a partner read it and answer the following revision and editing questions. You may also use this checklist to revise and edit your own paragraph.

Revising Paragraph Structure

☐ Does the topic sentence indicate that the paragraph is about the definition of a word? If not, what might you change?

☐ Underline the topic sentence. How is the definition stated (as a synonym, by negation, or by category)? Does the topic sentence indicate the pattern of development? What might you change or add?

☐ What pattern is used in the supporting and development sentences to explain or show the definition? Are all the elements for that pattern present?

☐ What transition words move you through the paragraph? Where might you make changes?

☐ Does the concluding sentence remind the reader of the definition of the term? Does it offer a final observation?

☐ What point of view is used throughout the paragraph? How relevant is it to the writer's purpose? Is it consistent throughout the paragraph? Are any changes needed?

☐ Is there a title? Is it catchy and reflective of the definition paragraph?

Editing Spelling, Diction, and Sentence Construction

☐ Are there any misspelled words?

☐ Are appropriate and specific words used?

☐ Are slang words, text message language, or clichés used?

☐ Consider the sentence structure and correct any errors with:

    ☐ Fragments, run-ons, and comma splices

    ☐ Misplaced or dangling modifiers

    ☐ Pronoun agreement

    ☐ Subject and verb agreement

Final Assessment

☐ What do you like the most about this paragraph?

☐ What are you unclear about or have difficulty with in this paragraph?

UNIT FOUR: Building an Essay from Paragraphs

Y OU CAN NOW use your knowledge of the writing patterns to turn paragraphs into essays. Essentially, an essay is a group of paragraphs on a single subject. When you write an essay, you follow the same prewriting and writing process you use when you write a paragraph; you begin with planning, narrowing, and organizing your ideas, then drafting ideas, and finally revising and editing. In the following chapter, you see how the techniques you learned for writing paragraphs can help you write essays. Chapter Eleven shows you the specific elements required for a cohesive and unified essay.

CHAPTER ELEVEN: Writing an Essay

Whereas a **paragraph** is a collection of **sentences,** an **essay** is a collection of **paragraphs**. Both paragraphs and essays are structured around three main parts. As you move from paragraph to essay, the name of each part changes:

A Paragraph		**An Essay**
Topic Sentence	⟷	Introduction Paragraph & Thesis Statement
Supporting Sentences	⟷	Supporting Paragraphs
Concluding Sentence	⟷	Conclusion Paragraph

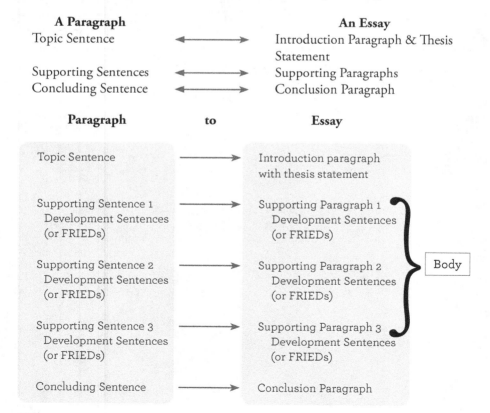

Paragraph	**to**	**Essay**	
Topic Sentence	⟶	Introduction paragraph with thesis statement	
Supporting Sentence 1 Development Sentences (or FRIEDs)	⟶	Supporting Paragraph 1 Development Sentences (or FRIEDs)	
Supporting Sentence 2 Development Sentences (or FRIEDs)	⟶	Supporting Paragraph 2 Development Sentences (or FRIEDs)	Body
Supporting Sentence 3 Development Sentences (or FRIEDs)	⟶	Supporting Paragraph 3 Development Sentences (or FRIEDs)	
Concluding Sentence	⟶	Conclusion Paragraph	

DRAFTING AN ESSAY

An **essay** is a collection of paragraphs, typically between four to six paragraphs, but it can vary in length depending on the assignment. The number of paragraphs is not as important as how these paragraphs function together to show the writer's opinion. In other words, the content conveyed in those paragraphs is most essential. An essay includes three types of paragraphs labeled as introduction paragraph, body paragraph, and conclusion paragraph. There is no perfect length for an essay, as it depends on the assignment and your purpose in writing.

✂ BUILDING TIP

Remember to consider your assignment, purpose, audience, and point of view when you set out to write an essay.

- Understand the specific requirements of your **assignment** as given to you by your instructor.

- Consider who will be reading your essay—your **audience**.

- Think about what you hope to share—your **purpose**—in writing your essay. Is your purpose to inform, entertain, inspire, or persuade?

- Determining your purpose helps you decide the **point of view** you will use throughout your essay.

  —If your purpose is to share a personal story, the point of view will be **first person** and use *I* or *we*.

  —If your purpose is to write instructions or how-to essays, the point of view will be **second person** and use *you* and *your*.

  —If you are explaining something from a detached position, the point of view will be **third person** and you will refer to your subjects by name or by pronouns such as *it, he, she, they, him, her,* and/or *them.*

While essays are generally composed of multiple paragraphs, in some college courses, a five-paragraph essay is required. The important thing to remember is that regardless of length, all essays include an introduction paragraph, body paragraphs, and a conclusion paragraph.

Introduction Paragraph

The **introduction paragraph** is the first paragraph in the essay, and its purpose is to introduce the reader to what the essay is about specifically. The length of the introduction can vary depending on your topic and purpose, and it accomplishes several things:

- Attracts or **"hooks"** the reader's attention
- Provides **specific remarks** about the subject
- States the **thesis statement** and may state the **forecasting statement**

An introduction moves the reader from general to specific ideas. It may begin with a sentence or sentences that introduce the discussion and "hook" the reader's attention, but by the end of the introductory paragraph, the reader should understand the essay's main focus. Generally, most introductions may follow this general diagram:

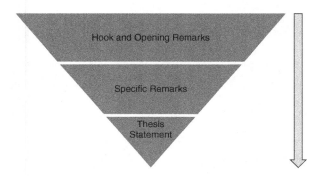

The Hook

The **hook** is a sentence or sentences at the beginning of introductory paragraph that start the discussion and attract the readers' attention, so they keep reading. There are a number of ways to write the hook to get the readers' attention:

1. **General scenario or historical background information.** You can offer several researched or common-knowledge factual sentences about your topic in the first sentences before your thesis statement.

> We have an Oscars ceremony once a year to tell rich people how great they are for standing in front of a camera for millions of dollars a week, playing roles of brave firemen or conscionable doctors. For entertaining the masses, they get paid exorbitant amounts of money and are given great recognition while those who truly risk their lives every day to keep others safe are not given a second glance. We should give awards to those who are real heroes every day who risk their lives for others.

2. **Definition.** You can start with a definition of a word that relates to your discussion. Consider the following opening sentences taken from a longer introductory paragraph:

> Actors are not true heroes. Heroes are real people who save lives regardless of the danger to their own safety.

3. **Quotation.** You can use a quote from someone famous; from an old saying; or from a slogan, song, or movie.

> According to William Shakespeare, "All the world's a stage, and all the men and women merely players; they have their exits and their entrances; and one man in his time plays many parts," so why not recognize these players on stage who entertain us with their heroic acting? After all, they may make their exits all too soon.

4. **Shocking statement or question.** In your first sentence, use a shocking statement or ask a question.

> Yesterday, my favorite movie hero died from a drug overdose. He left me wondering what I ever saw in him that was heroic. Should famous actors be recognized as heroes?

After the hook sentences are presented, you may offer a few common informational remarks about the specific topic of your essay and move the reader toward your main focus: the thesis statement.

Thesis Statement

The foundation of an effective essay is a strong thesis statement. The introduction includes a thesis statement, which indicates the essay's topic and the writer's specific opinion about the topic.

🪚 BUILDING TIP

The thesis statement offers an **opinion** or a narrowed focus about the topic, which is called the **focused topic** of the essay. The **focused topic** is what the writer will explain or show in the essay. Remember, a thesis statement is always a statement of opinion and never a statement of fact.

■ A **fact** is something that can be verified or proven.

■ An **opinion** is something that requires that its writer show you why he or she feels, believes, or thinks that way, because it is not based on fact and it is not verifiable.

You may place your thesis statement anywhere in the beginning or middle of the introduction, although generally it is placed at the end of the introduction after you have hooked the reader and given some specific remarks about your topic. Wherever you place your thesis statement, it should tell readers what to expect in your essay. A thesis statement in one sentence should:

- State your opinion or **focused topic** about the subject.
- Indicate what **writing pattern** is used for organizing supporting details.

 MEMORY TIP

Thesis Statement = Focused Topic (Opinion about Topic + Writing Pattern)

To write effective thesis statements, consider your purpose for the topic because that helps you determine how best to explain it to your readers. Ask yourself:

- What feelings or thoughts do I have about the topic?
- What kinds of thoughts about this topic do I want to share with my audience?
- How can I show the importance of the topic to others?
- How might the feelings of others differ from my own?

Prewriting helps significantly with this process because it allows you to explore and narrow your thoughts about the topic. By exploring your ideas, you may also discover the pattern of writing that best suits your essay's purpose. Once you have settled on a writing pattern and on your opinion about the topic, combine these two elements into one clear sentence that shows your focused topic. The following are examples of generic thesis statements about the topic of shoes. They are designed to show how you may state the thesis statement using the different writing patterns you learned in the previous chapters:

Illustration
During my workday, I change into several kinds of shoes.

Cause or Effect
Wearing good running shoes is important for several reasons.

Not wearing the right shoe during workouts results in several bad effects.

Classification

Based on where I wear shoes, my shoes can be grouped into three functional groups.

Comparison or Contrast

Nike and Adidas basketball shoes share several similarities.
The 1930s women's shoe styles differed from today's women's shoe styles.

Description

My red, sparkly shoes are my going-out shoes.

Narration

My experience buying shoes showed me the value of wisely investing my money.

Definition

Horseshoes are not omens of good luck.

You can mention the specific supporting ideas of your essay in a thesis, but that is not mandatory. Stating the supporting ideas in the thesis helps you lay out the specific plan for developing the body paragraphs and offers readers a prediction or projection of the supporting ideas. Because of its predicting nature, this sentence in the introduction is called the **forecasting statement** or **plan of development.**

Prewriting helps with the development of the forecasting statement. Through the process of exploring ideas about your topic, you may discover ideas you could use for supporting your focus. To decide on the points you may use in the forecasting statement, ask yourself:

- What kinds of ideas would best explain or support my opinion about the topic?
- What ideas may be relevant as support for my thesis?
- How might I organize these supporting ideas?
- Should I present a list of examples? A story? A comparison? A description? Specific examples? Which ones? A combined method of patterns?

Once you determine the pattern and the supporting ideas you could use for the thesis statement, organize these ideas into a logical order. Then, condense them into brief points, so you can list them. The list of supporting ideas is your forecasting statement. Often, it is combined with the thesis statement, although it may stand alone. Consider the following example:

Topic:	Water skiing
Opinion:	Learning to water ski is important to me
Writing pattern:	Reasons why I learned it
Supporting ideas:	All my friends ski
	Great way to exercise
	I love being in the water

How would you write the thesis with a forecasting statement for this topic? Use the supporting ideas that show the writing pattern and explain the opinion.

Without the supporting points or forecasting statement:

In my family, learning to water ski is important.

With the supporting points or forecasting statement:

I learned to water ski because all my family members water ski, it is a great way to exercise, and I love being in the water.

BUILDING SKILLS 11-1: Recognizing Effective Thesis Statements

Write *TS* next to the sentences that are effective thesis statements. Remember that a good thesis statement states the focused topic (writer's opinion about the topic) and indicates the pattern for development.

_____ 1. There are several reasons for making Election Day a national holiday.

_____ 2. My uncle thinks he is funny, but sometimes his humor can be offensive and vulgar.

_____ 3. Some television shows negatively portray women or minorities.

_____ 4. Playing on the high school football team has taught me a valuable lesson about honesty.

_____ 5. Sacramento is the capital of California.

_____ 6. Several similarities exist between the roles of a football quarterback and an army general.

_____ 7. Ocean life has four separate realms.

_____ 8. The word *macho* means manly and, in several cultures, it is an important attribute for males.

_____ 9. The rap genre of music can be classified into three groups based on the musical lyrics and message.

_____ 10. Shakespeare was a British writer.

BUILDING SKILLS: 11-2: Completing a Thesis Statement

Complete the following phrases to make each one a clear thesis statement. A topic and part of the focus is given, and the missing part may be more than one word.

1. An excellent doctor should _____

_____.

2. Working part-time while in college can create _____

_____.

3. Writing is _____for college students.

4. Giving advice to a friend who did not ask can _____

_____.

5. Borrowing money from a family member can _____

_____.

BUILDING SKILLS 11-3: Writing Effective Thesis Statements

Prewrite on each of the following topics; then draft a thesis statement for each topic. You may include forecasting statements as part of your thesis statements.

1. Inspiration

_____

_____

_____

_____

2. First impressions

_____

_____

_____

_____

3. Physical education

_____

_____

_____

_____

4. Perseverance

_____

_____

5. Environmentalism

_____

_____

_____

_____

BUILDING SKILLS 11-4: Supporting Sentences and Thesis Statements

Look at each list of supporting sentences and develop a thesis statement to fit each list.

1. a. Appropriate attire for an interview.
   b. Self-confidence during the interview.
   c. Enthusiasm about the job being interviewed for.

Thesis statement: _____

_____

2. a. Celebrities have little to no privacy.
    b. Celebrities get a high regard of themselves and become egotistical.
    c. Celebrities abuse substances to deal with the pressure.
Thesis statement: _____

_____

3. a. Arranged marriages achieve a strong link between two people.
    b. Arranged marriages provide the social and financial support for both families.
    c. Arranged marriages turn into love matches.
Thesis statement: _____

_____

When writing your introduction and thesis statements, follow these suggestions:

- **Avoid announcing, apologizing, or complaining about your writing intentions.** Do not use sentences that announce your intentions like this:

    In this essay, I will write about the need for better shopping stores. My purpose in writing this is to get you to see how unfair shopping can be to some.

    Do not use sentences that apologize about your intentions like this:

    Forgive me if I offend you with my opinion about shopping.

    Do not use sentences that complain about your topic like this:

    Even though shopping is not my favorite subject to discuss, I will still share with you my feelings about it.

- **Do not state the thesis statement *only* without introductory sentences.** If the thesis statement is the only sentence in the introduction then you do not have an introductory paragraph but just a statement of opinion. More importantly, you will not be able to capture the reader's attention and interest; therefore, your essay will be dismissed.
- **Avoid writing long introductions.** The length of an introduction varies, but be sure that it only introduces, not develops, ideas. Development is reserved for the supporting paragraphs in the body of the essay.

Consider this example for writing an essay's introductory paragraph with a thesis statement:

Do you have a minute? That may be all it takes to save the life of a child—your child. — *This is the hook— a question with a shocking statement.*

Each year, accidents at home kill many of our young children under the age of 15. In what should be the safest environment for children, home, ours are rushed to hospitals or die from ingesting pesticides, choking on simple hazards, or discovering hidden firearms. — *These are general remarks that offer background information.*

We do not have a minute to lose. Such deaths and injuries can be avoided through three easy steps parents can take right now. — *This is the thesis statement.*

BUILDING SKILLS 11-5: Thesis Statement Language

Each of the following sentences demonstrates one of three incorrect ways to write a thesis. Read each statement and write *A* next to those that announce; *AP* next to those that apologize; and *C* next to those that complain.

_____ 1. What to do during an earthquake is the subject of this essay.

_____ 2. I do not like the subject about music being effective for teaching children.

_____ 3. I humbly say I like Salem, the capital of Oregon.

_____ 4. I want to share with you that marrying in your twenties has many benefits.

_____ 5. In this essay, I will discuss teenage drinking.

_____ 6. I hope I do not offend my audience with my opinion on single parenthood.

_____ 7. Although I hate dogs, obedience training helps them in several ways.

_____ 8. To begin with, obesity is a serious problem among our nation's children.

_____ 9. It is my humble opinion that fresh pizza is better than frozen pizza.

_____ 10. While I am not fond of this subject, there are three problems for subscribers of magazines.

BUILDING SKILLS 11-6: Writing an Introduction

Pick one of the following two thesis statements and write an introductory paragraph, being sure to include a hook and a thesis statement in your paragraph. Two positions are offered for each thesis statement, so pick the one that suits your purpose.

1. The music industry has (or has not) changed because of new technologies.

_____

_____

_____

_____

_____

_____

_____

_____

_____

2. Winning the lottery would (or would not) change the way I live my life.

_____

_____

_____

_____

_____

_____

_____

_____

_____

Body: Supporting Paragraphs

The body of an essay is composed of supporting paragraphs the writer develops to explain the thesis statement. Supporting paragraphs are sometimes called body paragraphs because they make up the main part or body of the discussion that explains or shows the thesis statement. They should be unified or related to the thesis. They should also be coherent in that they flow smoothly and logically. You may use as many supporting paragraphs as you feel you need to explain your thesis statement, but, generally, college-level essays include two to five supporting paragraphs. Each supporting paragraph includes the following:

1. **Topic sentence:** The topic sentence in a paragraph within an essay is not one of opinion but one that expresses the main idea to be developed in each body or supporting paragraph. It tells the reader what point will be explained in each body or supporting paragraph. Generally, it may be the first sentence for each supporting paragraph; however, it may be placed in the middle or at the end of the supporting paragraph. Topic sentences achieve unity—agreement or harmony—among the ideas to advance or prove the opinion in the thesis.

2. **Development sentences**: These are informational sentences that come after the topic sentence and provide details about the topic. Development sentences help the reader understand your topic sentence. Because development sentences clarify, explain, or make it easier for readers to remember the main idea in each supporting paragraph, they should contain a variety of information such as facts about the topic sentence, reasons for the topic sentence, examples for the topic sentence, or details to clarify the topic sentence and help the reader accept each important point in your essay. As the writer, you choose what specific information points to use to explain your topic sentences. Development information comes from many sources and depends on your audience and your purpose for writing. Personal experience, observations, facts, statistics, case studies, or memories and more can help you make your topic sentences clear and convincing. There is no set length, no prescribed number of lines or sentences for development sentences. They need to be long enough to accomplish their purpose of explaining each topic sentence and short enough to be interesting.

3. **Unity and coherence:** These elements are essential for the flow of logic between and within body paragraphs. They solidify the support for the thesis statement and help create a logical, clear, and organized essay.
   - □ Unity means agreement: In essay writing, agreement comes in the form of supporting paragraphs that present and explain ideas that relate directly to the thesis statement. Select and communicate supporting ideas that connect to or agree with the opinion in your topic sentence. Most importantly, uniting or linking the supporting paragraphs to the thesis statement increases your credibility or believability as a writer. Every sentence in the body of the essay supports the opinion stated in the thesis statement.
   - □ Coherence means consistent or clear. In essay writing, consistency and clarity help the writer's ideas flow smoothly and logically. Coherence requires the supporting paragraphs to be organized in a particular manner to move the reader from one supporting paragraph to another or from idea to idea within each paragraph. To achieve coherence

within and between supporting paragraphs, transitional words or expressions/phrases are essential.

4. **Transitions**: These are words or expressions used to help the reader keep up with the flow and logic of thoughts. Transitions create coherence in an essay because they show how the supporting paragraphs have been arranged, or ordered. The most common orders are:
   - □ time or chronological order (first, second, third . . .)
   - □ spatial order (in front, next to, behind . . .)
   - □ importance or emphatic order (least to most important)

In organizing your body paragraphs, it is important to use transitions to move the reader through your sequence of supporting ideas. Transitions also help you indicate the writing pattern you have decided to use. Generally, the pattern of writing you use to develop your thesis statement determines the transitions you use to move through the body paragraph's supporting ideas.

✂ BUILDING TIP

Here are some examples of the most common transitions you may use to help order your body paragraphs.

Writing Pattern	Common Transitions
Illustration	First example
	Second example
	Most important example
Cause or Effect	First cause (or effect)
	Second cause (or effect)
	Third cause (or effect)
Classification	First group
	Second group
	Third group
Comparison or Contrast Point-by-point	First similarity (or difference)
	Subject A
	Subject B
	Another similarity (or difference)
	Subject A
	Subject B

➡

🛠 BUILDING TIP (*Continued*)

	A third similarity (or difference)
	Subject A
	Subject B
Comparison and Contrast	Subject A
Topic-by-topic	First, second, third points of similarity or difference
	Subject B
	First, second, third points of similarity or difference
Description	Organize sensory details by order of time or space
	In front, next, behind, at the back
	In the beginning, then, next, last
Narration	Tell a story by organizing the experience using the BCOOL (background, conflict, order of events, outcome, lesson) pattern.
Definition	Organize by using *one or a combination* of the previous patterns.

Refer to Appendix B for a complete list of transitions.

BUILDING SKILLS 11-7: Creating Supporting Sentences

For each thesis, write three topic sentences to serve as supporting paragraphs for the thesis.

1. Thesis: In my family, we have three unique traditions for celebrating special occasions.

   Topic sentence for supporting paragraph 1: _____
   _____
   _____

Topic sentence for supporting paragraph 2: _____
_____
_____

Topic sentence for supporting paragraph 3: _____
_____
_____

2. Thesis: Based on how often I see them, my friends can be classified into several categories.

Topic sentence for supporting paragraph 1: _____
_____
_____

Topic sentence for supporting paragraph 2: _____
_____
_____

Topic sentence for supporting paragraph 3: _____
_____
_____

BUILDING SKILLS 11-8: Writing Supporting Paragraphs

Select one of the introductions you wrote for Building Skills 11-6 and write a supporting paragraph that explains your thesis statement. You could write more than one supporting paragraph; however, be sure to develop fully your supporting idea.

Topic and introduction chosen:
_____
_____
_____

Supporting paragraph 1:
_____
_____
_____

_____
_____
_____
_____
_____
_____
_____
_____
_____
_____
_____
_____

Conclusion Paragraph

The conclusion paragraph is the last paragraph in the essay and is designed to bring the discussion to a satisfying close. It should give the reader the feeling that you have said all you want to say about your topic. It is your last chance to persuade readers of your point of view or to impress yourself upon them as a writer and thinker. Its function is primarily to establish a sense of closure. It should be brief but may summarize the supporting paragraphs' topic sentences in the order they were presented as well as reword the thesis statement. To end an essay, consider using any or all of the following methods:

- Restate the thesis statement in different words.
- Make a final observation about the focused topic and/or supporting paragraphs.
- Close with a thoughtful remark about the topic.
- Summarize the supporting paragraphs in the body of your essay.

👆 MEMORY TIP

Use this acronym to remember the methods for concluding an essay: **RORS.**

Restating

Observing

Remarking

Summarizing

In you conclusion, you want to leave your readers with a **memorable impression** about your topic and thesis statement. A memorable impression is an unforgettable or noteworthy thought or idea in relation to your essay's discussion that lingers in the reader's mind. There are several ways to create memorable impressions:

- A prediction.

> In the next ten years, we will continue to hear about new bad driving laws.

- Quotation.

> In the words of Gilbert Parker, "Nothing is so unproductive as the law. It is expensive whether you win or lose."

- Recommendation/suggestion.

> Drivers should be appreciative of the new driving laws as they help protect their safety and the safety of others on the road.

- A call to action—the reader should do something.

> We should appreciate our country for providing us with laws that increase our driving safety.

You should avoid the following in your conclusion:

- **Announcing your conclusion.** Do not use sentences that announce you are closing your discussion; if you do, the readers will not bother reading your conclusion because you are telling them instead of showing them. Avoid sentences like:

> I would like to conclude this discussion with this statement: We should repeal the laws.

- **Complaining or apologizing about the assignment.** Do not include sentences about your view of the essay assignment like:

> Well, this is my humble opinion on the matter, and I am sorry if I have confused you with my thoughts.

> Although this is not my favorite subject to discuss, I will tell you how I feel about it.

- **Presenting an afterthought or new idea.** Do not add something you forgot to discuss in the body of the paper. That leaves the reader feeling unsatisfied with your discussion.

Consider this example of a conclusion paragraph:

To prevent curious children from household dangers or death, invest in child-proof cabinet locks, covers for electric outlets, and firearm safes. *Restatement of main ideas and thesis statement*

Of course, we cannot protect children from everything or foresee all the possible household dangers they may face, but with a little child safety planning and a lot of love, we can protect them from a lot. After all, one of the main responsibilities for parents is to provide safe environments for children. *Suggestion or recommendation*

Title

The same conventions apply to titles of essays as they do for titling paragraphs. Remember, titles should be:

- Reflective of your overall discussion
- Catchy, original, and short
- Capitalized

Your title should not have:

- Periods at the end, underlines, or quotation marks
- The name of the assignment

EXAMPLE PARAGRAPH TO ESSAY

My People's Influence

Paragraph

There are several people who have influenced me as I pursued my educational goals. The first person is my older sister, Char. She is always willing to help me when I need it: in fact, I always have her re-read the papers that I have to write. She always gives good advice that makes my papers more interesting. She used to be upset at me for my grammatical errors, but now she is amazed that I write so well. Another person who has influenced me has been my high school sports coach, Miguel. He always asks me how I'm doing in my schoolwork, and if I tell him that I'm getting a C in one of my classes, he asks me how I'm going to bring that grade up. Since he has been my coach, he has ways of making me try harder in my studies. If I need any help with anything, even outside of school, he is there to help me out. I know that he will do his best to help me when I need any help. The most influential person who has helped me in accomplishing my educational goals is my girlfriend, Laura. She has pushed me the most in my studies. She picks me up when I'm down on myself and when I stress out. She will tell me if my writing sounds catchy or not, so I can make corrections as needed. She's there to keep me in check. In addition, she is always there to give me a big hug and words of encouragement. My sister, coach, and my girlfriend are the people who have influenced me in the pursuit of my educational goals.

Supporting sentence 1 with a transition

Supporting sentence 2 with a transition

Supporting sentence 3 with a transition

Concluding sentence

Essay

Many people do not understand how difficult pursuing an education can be, and many families take no pride in their loved ones' education. On the other hand, some regard education as a high accomplishment and take great interest in their loved one's education. I am lucky in having my family's and friends' great support, and, along the way, several people have become great influences on the pursuit of my education.

The first person to influence me is my older sister, Char. She is a graduate of Cal Poly, Pomona, with dual degrees in Business and Agriculture. Despite her dyslexia, she was able to accomplish a lot in her life, and she is my inspiration. She is always willing to help me when I need it: in fact, I always have her re-read my papers that I have to write. She always gives me good advice that makes my papers more interesting. She used to get on me for my grammatical errors a lot, but since I've taken English classes in college, she is amazed at how well I write now.

Another person who has influenced me has been my high school sports coach, Miguel. He always asks me how I'm doing in my schoolwork, and if I tell him that I'm getting a "C" in one of my classes, he asks me how I'm going to bring that grade up. He is my mentor, and to him education is the key to a better life and a wise mind. Since he's been my coach, he has ways of making me try harder in my studies. If I need any help with

Thesis statement

Supporting paragraph 1 with transitions and FRIEDs

Supporting paragraph 2 with transitions and FRIEDs

anything, even outside of school, he is there to help me out. He always reminds me of the promise I made to him about finishing my bachelor's degree.

Supporting paragraph 3 with transitions and FRIEDs

The most influential person who has helped me in accomplishing my educational goals is my girlfriend, Laura. She's had a hard life as an orphan but through it all, her focus never wavered, and she accomplished her goal. She just finished her degree in nursing after years of working two jobs to pay her tuition. She understands how hard it can be sometimes, but she has pushed me the most in my studies. She picks me up when I'm down on myself and when I stress out. She will help me study for tests or tell me if my writing sounds catchy or not, so I can make corrections as needed. She's there to keep me in check. In addition, she is always there to give me a big hug and words of encouragement.

Restatement of thesis

I am fortunate to have my sister, coach, and girlfriend as the people who have influenced me in the pursuit of my educational goals. They have made it easier for me to achieve academically. In the words of George Eliot,

Memorable impression

"What do we live for, if it is not to make life less difficult to each other?"

BUILDING SKILLS 11-9: Expanding a Paragraph into an Essay

Choose one of your previously graded paragraphs as a rough draft for an essay. Rewrite and expand the graded paragraph into a five-paragraph essay. Be sure to add a strong introduction and thesis statement, expand on the supporting and development sentences, to develop a thoughtful conclusion. To draft your essay, refer to the example of Paragraph to Essay at the beginning of this chapter.

BUILDING SKILLS 11-10: Creating Outlines for Essays

Select one of the thesis statements you developed in Building Skills 11-3 or Building Skills 11-6. On a separate sheet of paper, use that thesis statement to compose a formal or informal outline for an essay. Refer to the beginning of this chapter for an overview of an essay's parts. Also refer to Chapter One for a thorough explanation on outlines.

BUILDING SKILLS TOGETHER 11-1: Evaluating an Essay

Working in a small group, read the following essay and answer the evaluation questions that follow.

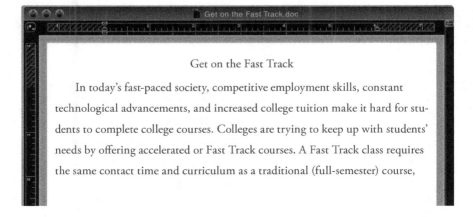

Get on the Fast Track

In today's fast-paced society, competitive employment skills, constant technological advancements, and increased college tuition make it hard for students to complete college courses. Colleges are trying to keep up with students' needs by offering accelerated or Fast Track courses. A Fast Track class requires the same contact time and curriculum as a traditional (full-semester) course, but its length of time is cut in half. For example, at some colleges, English courses can be offered in eight weeks rather than the traditional sixteen weeks, so students are able to enroll in two English courses during one semester. Fast Track courses produce three positive outcomes for college students.

One outcome of Fast Track courses is increased retention of course information. Students are in daily contact because Fast Track classes meet Monday through Thursday for eight weeks per course instead of the typical one day or two days a week for traditional courses. Less time between class sessions raises the frequency for reviewing concepts and reduces the rate of information leakage. Therefore, material learned in an English class stays "fresh" in the students' minds, and they have better recollection for what they learned.

Another outcome of Fast Track courses is more student connections and community building in the classroom. In Fast Track classes, students see each other daily with the same instructor. This frequency leads to an informal environment that creates a sense of belonging, of attachment, and of bonding among the classmates and the instructor. The strong rapport with the teacher and classmates helps students feel secure and comfortable with the class environment. Therefore, they are more likely to make friends with classmates and to participate in class.

The third outcome of Fast Track courses is the speed of completing courses. The daily contact and strong connections with others encourages students to attend class. Consistent attendance enhances the rate at which students persist or continue in the class. Course persistence, along with the short time span of a Fast Track course, pushes students to complete coursework faster and to move on to the next Fast Track course. Therefore, students are likely to complete more than one course in one semester.

Fast Track classes help raise course material retention, student connections, and completion rates. Many students want a sense of belonging and a reason for persistence in college, especially in these times of challenging employment and economic times and constant technological advancements. The best track for college students may just be the Fast Track.

1. Is the introduction clear and appealing? How does it capture the attention of the reader? Does it offer sufficient introductory sentences about the topic?

   _____

   _____

2. Underline the thesis statement. Does it include a strong focused topic? If so, what is it? Is a clear pattern of writing stated? If so, what is it?

   _____

   _____

3. How many supporting paragraphs are provided? Are they stated in a particular order?

   _____

   _____

4. Do the supporting paragraphs provide strong support or explanation of the thesis statement? Why or why not?

   _____

   _____

5. Is each supporting paragraph sufficiently developed with enough development sentences (or FRIEDs)? Explain your answer.

   _____

   _____

6. What, if any, transitions are used to move the reader through the body paragraphs? List them and determine the order they show.

   _____

   _____

7. Is there a conclusion paragraph? How does it end the essay's discussion? Does it offer a final observation or memorable impression? How? Explain your answer.

   _____

   _____

8. State the point of view (first, second, or third person) used in this essay. Is it effective for the writer's purpose? Is it used consistently throughout?

   _____

   _____

9. What do you think of the title? Is it catchy? Is it reflective of what the essay discusses?

_____

_____

SUGGESTED TOPICS FOR ESSAYS

Choose one of the following topics or use one of your own and then use prewriting techniques to develop your essay draft.

Airport security	Greed
Fashion stereotypes	Pride
Terrorism	Apologies
Anxiety	Best or worst inventions in the last 50 years

◆ BUILDING SKILLS TOGETHER 11-2: Essay Feedback ▌ Checklist

Once the rough draft of your essay is completed, have a partner read it and answer the following revision and editing questions. You may also use this checklist to revise and edit your own essay.

Revising Essay Structure

☐ Does the introduction capture the reader's attention? Are there sufficient and interesting introductory sentences before the thesis statement? What changes might you make?

☐ Underline the thesis statement. Does it include an opinion or focused topic and an indication of the writing pattern? What changes might you make?

☐ How many supporting paragraphs are used? Are they organized logically with clear topic sentences? What changes might you make?

☐ Is each supporting paragraph sufficiently explained with enough development sentences (or FRIEDs)? What might you change?

☐ Are transition words used to move you through the body paragraphs? Is there a clear order of thoughts? Where might you make changes?

☐ Does the conclusion summarize the supporting paragraphs, restate the thesis statement, or offer a strong memorable impression or thoughtful observation? What changes might you make?

☐ What point of view is used in the essay? How relevant is it to the writer's purpose? Is it consistent throughout the essay? Are any changes needed?

☐ Is there a title? Is it catchy and reflective of the overall essay? Is it effective?

Editing Spelling, Diction, and Sentence Construction

☐ Are there any misspelled words?

☐ Are appropriate and specific words used?

☐ Are slang words, text message language, or clichés used?

☐ Consider the sentence structure and correct any errors with:

  ☐ Fragments, run-ons, and comma splices

  ☐ Misplaced or dangling modifiers

  ☐ Pronoun agreement

  ☐ Subject and verb agreement

Final Assessment

☐ What do you like the most about this essay?

☐ What are you unclear about or have difficulty with in this essay?

APPENDIX A: Basic Grammar

If you are building a house, you will need sand, gravel, water, and cement to form the concrete foundation of your home. You may have these ingredients on hand, or you may have to go and find them. In writing, grammar rules are essential ingredients to the foundation of a good sentence, paragraph, or essay. You may have these rules already learned and ready to use—or you may have to go and find them. Many of the basic rules can be found in this appendix. Fuller explanations, exercises, and additional rules can be found in the companion to this book: *Building Better Grammar*. The definitions and rules are organized into three categories: completeness, consistency, and clarity.

I: BE COMPLETE

Parts of Speech

Every word you write or speak falls into one of eight categories or types. These are collectively called the **parts of speech**. The eight parts of speech are nouns, pronouns, verbs, adjectives, adverbs, prepositions, conjunctions, and interjections.

Nouns

The **noun** names a person, place, thing, or idea. Often, nouns are preceded by the article adjectives *the, a,* and *an.*

The <u>dog</u>
A <u>girl</u>
An <u>ant</u>
The <u>sky</u> is blue.
<u>Hurricanes</u> terrify me.
Their <u>belief</u> in the <u>right</u> of all <u>human beings</u> to live in <u>peace</u> is what motivates the <u>protestors</u>.

Pronouns

Pronouns take the place of nouns. They serve two functions:

1. **To avoid excessive repetition.**
   Manny calls Manny's teacher to tell the teacher that Manny will be late.
   Manny calls <u>his</u> teacher to tell <u>her</u> that <u>he</u> will be late.
2. **To refer to something or someone that is not specifically identified.**
   <u>Something</u> is bothering me.
   Why didn't you tell <u>anyone</u>?

The noun that a pronoun replaces is called the **antecedent**. Pronouns that refer to a clearly identified antecedent are called **definite pronouns**.

I, me, my, myself	he, him, his, himself
they, them, their, themselves	you, your, yourselves
she, her, hers, herself	we, us, our, ours, ourselves
who, whose, which, what	that, this, these, those
it, its, itself	

Pronouns that refer to a noun that is <u>not</u> clearly identified are called **indefinite pronouns**.

anything	nothing	something	everything
anyone	no one	someone	everyone
each	either	neither	many
few	some	must	

Verbs

Verbs show action or show a state of being.

Action verbs: some examples are *play, eat, talk, jump,* and *dance.*
   I <u>walk</u> home.
   The bells <u>jangled</u>.

Being verbs: these verbs are identified by the verb *to be: is, am, are, was, were, will be.*

I <u>am</u> a mother.

He <u>is</u> a monster.

Any of the forms of *be* (*am, is, was, were*) and also some other verbs can be used as **helping verbs**. Helping verbs come before the main verb to refine and clarify the exact nature and timing of the action.

He <u>is going</u> to the mall.

We <u>had helped</u> every time until now.

It <u>will be raining</u> soon.

Helping Verbs in Addition to *Be*			
do	does	did	have
has	had	shall	should
will	would	can	could
may	might	must	

Verbs change form according to when an action occurs; these changing verb forms are called **verb tenses**. Verb tenses help us track subjects and sentences in time:

Past
(All time before now)
The baby <u>talked</u>.

Present
(Now)
The baby <u>talks</u>.

Future
(All time beyond now)
The baby <u>will talk</u>.

Within each of these three tenses, there are four additional tenses that allow a writer to describe extremely specific times in which things happen. There are twelve tenses in all:

	Simple	Perfect	Progressive	Perfect Progressive
Present	She writes.	She has written.	She is writing.	She has been writing.
Past	She wrote.	She had written.	She was writing.	She had been writing.
Future	She will write.	She will have written.	She will be writing.	She will have been writing.

Adjectives and Adverbs

Adjectives and adverbs provide further description, identification, or limitation to the meaning of other words. They have similar properties, so adjectives and adverbs are often grouped together as **descriptors** or **modifiers**. What is the difference between them? **Adjectives** modify nouns and pronouns. They answer the questions: *Which one? What kind?* and *How many?*

The scientist photographed <u>red-winged</u> blackbirds.

I was delighted to see the <u>beautiful</u> blackbirds up close.

There were <u>ten</u> blackbirds.

Adverbs modify verbs, adjectives, and other adverbs, and they answer questions like *How? Where? When?* and *To what degree?*

He answered <u>quickly</u>.
They flew <u>south</u>.
The ship sailed <u>last week</u>.
She was <u>somewhat</u> angry.

Adjectives and adverbs come in three degrees: positive, comparative, and superlative. The **positive form** makes no comparison; the **comparative form** makes a comparison between two things; and the **superlative form** distinguishes among three or more things.

We go to an <u>old</u> school. (positive)
It is <u>older</u> than the state college. (comparative)
It is the <u>oldest</u> college in the Southwest. (superlative)

Prepositions

Prepositions are words that help signal a place (*above, inside, behind*), time (*before, after, within*), or source (*to, from, for, of, by*). Prepositions show the relationship between a noun or pronoun—called the **object** of the preposition—and other words in the sentence. Many words that are commonly used as prepositions may also function as adverbs or other parts of speech.

I looked <u>up</u> the street.
The bell rang <u>before</u> the teacher finished talking.
Did you get that <u>from</u> an online store?

Consult this list for more prepositions:

Place		Time	Source	
above	across	after	about	against
among	around	before	at	by
below	behind	during	because of	due to
beneath	beside	until	except	for
between	beyond	since	from	of
by	in/into		off	to
inside	near		toward	with
out	outside		without	
over	on			
through	under			
up	upon			
within				

Conjunctions

Conjunctions are words that join two or more clauses with one another. There are three kinds of conjunctions: coordinating, subordinating, and conjunctive adverbs.

1. **Coordinating conjunctions** link independent clauses. An easy way to remember these conjunctions is by using the acronym FANBOYS. The acronym includes the first letter of each of the seven coordinating conjunctions.

, for	and	, nor	, but	, or	, yet	, so

I like milk, <u>but</u> I prefer hot chocolate with breakfast.

2. **Subordinating conjunctions** link independent clauses with dependent clauses.

after	before	so that	whenever
although	because	provided that	where
as	even though	rather than	whereas
as if	if	until	whether
as long as	once	unless	while
as though	since	when	

I like my job <u>even though</u> I am not satisfied with the salary.
<u>Although</u> she is in pain, she is not letting it show.

3. **Adverbial conjunctions** link independent clauses.

; also,	; therefore,	; otherwise,	; consequently,
; besides,	; nonetheless,	; furthermore,	; nevertheless,
; instead,	; however,	; for instance,	; accordingly,
; indeed,	; moreover,	; likewise,	; for example,
; in fact,	; as a result,	; in addition,	; meanwhile,
; thus,	; then,	; similarly,	; hence,
; on the other hand,	; subsequently,		

He was finished with the project; <u>therefore</u>, he went home.

Interjections

Interjections are words that show surprise or emotion.

Hey, stop that please.

When an interjection appears alone, it is usually followed with an exclamation mark.

Wow!   Cowabunga!   Finally!

Parts of a Sentence

A sentence must contain a subject and a verb; without either one of these parts, a sentence is incomplete and will confuse the reader.

Subject

The **subject** is the part of the sentence that tells the reader who or what is doing or being something in the sentence.

<u>Mary</u> spoke.

[Mary is the subject of this sentence.]

Subjects can ONLY be nouns or pronouns, though these may be made up of multiple words.

<u>The daughter of my father's best friend</u> spoke.

<u>Someone who shall remain nameless</u> spoke.

Taken together, all the words that name or modify the subject are called the **complete subject**. There are three other ways to refer to a sentence's subject:

1. **Simple subject.** When a sentence has one noun or pronoun doing the action, that sentence has one subject known as a simple subject.

   <u>Daniel</u> plays the drums.

   Who plays the drums?

   Daniel ← 1 noun

   Because there is one subject, it is called a simple subject.

2. **Compound subject.** When a sentence has two or more nouns or pronouns doing the same action, they are collectively referred to as a compound subject.

   <u>Daniel and Marty</u> play the drums.

   Who plays the drums?

   Daniel and Marty ← 2 nouns

3. **Implied subject.** Sometimes a sentence does not directly state its subject, but it is clear that one exists.

   Come to the meeting to learn about the new tax laws.

   Here, the subject can be understood to be "you." Commands like this have the implied subject "you."

Verb

The second essential part of a sentence is the **verb**. Both the subject and verb can be one word or many.

1. The **simple verb** is the main verb of the sentence.

   Daniel <u>plays</u> the drums.

2. The **complete verb** includes not only the main verb but also all words that modify or directly relate to it.

   Daniel <u>plays the drums fast enough to blow us away</u>.

3. A **compound verb** occurs in a sentence where more than one verb has the same subject.

   Daniel <u>plays</u> the drums, <u>writes</u> the songs, and <u>produces</u> the recordings.

Objects of Verbs

Some verbs require a **direct object**, a word or words that indicate who or what received the action of the verb.

The record company pays its <u>songwriters</u> less than they deserve.

Without the direct object *songwriters* and its modifiers, this sentence—"The record company pays"—would be incomplete. You would ask, *Whom* or *what does the company pay?* Asking a *Whom?* or *What?* question about the verb of a sentence is a good way to find its direct object.

An **indirect object** is a person or thing to whom (or for whom) the action of the verb is directed. It must be a noun or a pronoun that comes before the direct object.

Laura handed <u>Jerry</u> the keys.

(direct object=the keys; indirect object=Jerry)

To whom did Laura hand the keys? To Jerry. The keys is the direct object and Jerry is the indirect object of the verb *handed*.

Phrases

A phrase is a group of related words lacking a subject, a verb, or both. A phrase can function as a verb.

Her family <u>has been having</u> a difficult year.

A phrase can function as a noun.

<u>The board of trustees</u> blocked the motion.

A phrase can function as a modifier to the noun or verb.

My mom, <u>a lifelong hypochondriac</u>, is in bed again. (phrase modifies noun)
The new teacher arrived <u>long before the students</u>. (phrase modifies verb)

Clauses

It is important to understand the difference between a **sentence** and a **clause**. Both are grammatical labels for a group of words that <u>must</u> contain a subject and a verb. A sentence, however, <u>may</u> contain more than one subject/verb groups; in other words, a sentence may consist of one, two, or more clauses. Consider these examples:

I own a beautiful cat.	Number of sentences: 1 Number of clauses: 1
I own a beautiful cat; her fur is glossy black, and after I brush it, her eyes glow with pleasure and she snuggles in my arms with loud purrs of contentment.	Number of sentences: 1 Number of clauses: 4

You can break down the longer sentence into separate clauses by underlining the subject (noun or pronoun) and verb (action or state of being) in each clause.

<u>I own</u> a beautiful cat
her <u>fur is</u> glossy black
after <u>I brush</u> it
her <u>eyes glow</u> with pleasure
<u>she snuggles</u> in my arms with loud purrs of contentment

There are two kinds of clauses: independent and dependent. Learning to arrange and connect clauses of differing completeness and purpose will help you create and punctuate complex sentences without confusing your reader.

Independent Clauses

An **independent clause** has a subject and a verb and expresses a complete thought. As its name suggests, an independent clause is a complete sentence that can stand by itself and does not need more information to give it meaning.

Dan laughed.

Dan is the subject and *laughed* is the verb. Do you need to know more? Not really. You might want to know what made Dan laugh, where he is and who he is with, or whether his laugh was happy or bitter—but these pieces of information are not essential for understanding what the sentence means. Grammatically, all that matters is that the sentence has a subject and a verb and that it makes sense on its own. *Dan laughed,* therefore, is an independent clause.

Dependent Clauses

A **dependent clause** has a subject and a verb but does not express a complete thought. As its name suggests, a dependent clause is *dependent on* more information to give it meaning. It cannot stand on its own as a complete sentence. The dependent clause is also referred to as a subordinate clause since it starts with a subordinating conjunction.

When Dan laughs.

Although *Dan* is the subject and *laughs* is the verb, you need to know more to make a complete statement. What happens when Dan laughs? Does someone smile or get mad at him? Do other people join him? You need more information to complete the meaning of this clause. Adding another clause will provide the needed information.

When Dan laughs, the walls shake and the baby wakes up from his nap.

When Dan laughs, therefore, is a dependent clause. Notice that the dependent clause in the example was created by the addition of an opening word (*when*) which told the reader to wait for additional information.

Use these conjunctions to show logical relationships of meaning:

Addition:
and, both...and, also, besides, furthermore, moreover
Contrast:
but, yet, however, instead, nevertheless, otherwise, similarly
Choice:
or, nor, either...or
Effect:
so, accordingly, consequently, therefore, thus
Substitution:
not...but
Sequence:
first, meanwhile, next, then, finally
Emphasis:
indeed, certainly

Use these subordinating conjunctions to show logical relationships of meaning:

Cause and Effect:
as, because, since, so that, in order that, in order to
Condition:
if, even if, unless, if only
Contrast:
although, even though, though
Comparison:
than, as though, as if, whereas, while
Choice:
whether, than, rather than
Sequence:
after, as, as long as, as soon as, before, once, since, until, when, whenever, while
Space:
where, wherever
Time:
when, whenever

Kinds of Sentences

The Simple Sentence

A **simple sentence** consists of a single independent clause.

I ate cake.

A simple sentence never has more than one clause (subject + verb), but that clause may contain compound subjects and verbs.

T.J. and Richy ate all the cake.

Mona and the kids finished off the punch and cookies.

Everybody cleared the dishes, turned off the lights, and locked the door.

The Compound Sentence

A **compound sentence** contains two or more independent clauses. Each clause, when viewed alone, can stand on its own as a sentence without changes or additions.

I ate cake, and my girlfriend ate cookies.

[I ate cake] and [my girlfriend ate cookies.]

The independent clauses in a compound sentence can be joined together by the following two types of conjunctions: **coordinating** and **adverbial,** both of which require punctuation. You can also choose to join two independent clauses using a stand-alone semicolon.

I ate cake, but my girlfriend ate cookies. (comma + coordinating conjunction)

I ate cake; however, my girlfriend ate cookies. (comma + adverbial conjunction)

I ate cake; my girlfriend ate cookies. (semi-colon)

The Complex Sentence

The **complex sentence** consists of one independent clause and one or more dependent clauses. Remember that a dependent clause has a subject and a verb but does not express a complete thought; it cannot stand on its own as a complete sentence. Because a dependent clause by its very nature is subordinate or inferior to an independent clause, the only option for connecting clauses in a complex sentence is a **subordinating conjunction.** If the dependent clause comes before the independent clauses, separate the clauses with a comma.

<u>If</u> she has a choice between cookies and cake, my girlfriend will choose cookies.

(dependent clause + independent clause)

If the dependent clause follows an independent clause, NO comma is needed.

<u>She will choose cookies</u> if they contain chocolate chips.

(independent clause + dependent clause)

The Compound-Complex Sentence

The **compound-complex sentence** consists of two or more independent clauses and one or more dependent clauses.

My father encouraged me to pick up a hobby, so I started collecting stamps; I became rich when I started a company that acquires and sells rare stamps; consequently, my hobby is now my livelihood.

This sentence is really five simple sentences combined together through the use of conjunctions and a semicolon.

II: BE CONSISTENT

Subject-Verb Agreement

Because subjects and verbs must be present in every grammatically complete sentence, they have a strong relationship with one another. When the two elements do not agree, the sentence stumbles, as in these examples:

Dogs is my favorite animals.

Jim eat a hamburger nearly every day.

One of the most precious resources in the United States are water.

In each of these sentences, the subject and verb disagree in number. In order to agree, a verb must follow the form of its subject in number:

1. If the subject is singular, the verb must be singular.
   My brother plays football.
2. If the subject is plural, the verb must be plural.
   My brothers play football.

Notice that in both sample sentences only one –*s* appears:

My brother plays football.

My brothers play football.

As a general rule, a singular verb ends in –*s*; a singular noun does not; a plural noun ends in –*s*; a plural verb does not.

This rule applies, however, only to regular verbs. Irregular verbs change form entirely according to number and person. The most troublesome irregular verbs for subject-verb agreement are *to be*, *to do*, and *to have*.

Irregular Verb Subject-Verb Agreement					
To be		**To do**		**To have**	
Present	**Past**	**Present**	**Past**	**Present**	**Past**
I am	I was	I do	I did	I have	I had
You are	You were	You do	You did	You have	You had
He/she/ it is	He/she/ it was	He/she/ it does	He/she/ it did	He/she/ it has	He/she/ it had
We are	We were	We do	We did	We have	We had
They are	They were	They do	They did	They have	They had

To be successful at subject-verb agreement, always locate the subject first and determine its number, then judge whether the present tense verb agrees with it. If the subject is singular, the verb should have an –s added to it to match its singular form. If the subject is plural (often ending in –s), the verb should not have an –s.

1. **Singular subjects can be:**

   a. Simple or singular.
      A <u>student</u> (talk, talks).
      <u>He or she</u> talks.
      A student <u>talks</u>.

   b. A collective noun. Test by replacing it with the pronoun *it*.
      The <u>team</u> (play, plays).
      <u>It</u> plays.
      The team <u>plays</u>.

   c. Subjects stating amount (time, money, measurement, weight, volume, fractions) are usually singular when the amount is considered as a unit. Test by replacing with the singular pronoun *it*.
      <u>Six dollars</u> (is, are) enough for the movie.
      <u>It</u> is enough.
      Six dollars <u>is</u> enough.

   d. An indefinite pronoun—*everyone, everybody, everything,* and *each.* Test by replacing it with the singular pronouns *he/she/it.*
      <u>Each</u> student (talk, talks).
      <u>He or she</u> talks.
      Each student <u>talks</u>.

2. **Plural subjects can be:**

   a. Simple and plural. Test by replacing with the plural pronouns *we* or *they*.
      The <u>students</u> (talk, talks).
      <u>We</u> talk.
      <u>They</u> talk.
      The students <u>talk</u>.

   b. Compound (two or more subjects). Test by replacing with the plural pronoun *they*.
      The <u>students and the teacher</u> (talk, talks).
      <u>They</u> talk.
      The students and the teacher <u>talk</u>.

c. An indefinite pronoun—*several, few, both, many.* Test by replacing it with the plural pronouns *we/they.*
  <u>Many</u> (talk, talks).
  <u>We</u> talk.
  <u>They</u> talk.
  Many <u>talk</u>.

Pronoun-Antecedent Agreement

Just as a verb must agree with its subject, so a pronoun must agree with the noun it replaces. That noun—called the **antecedent**—has a recognizable point of view, number, and gender. The pronoun reference has to agree with the **person, number,** or **gender** of the antecedent.

Pronoun Agreement with Person

If the antecedent is a person, then agreement can be achieved by using the pronouns *he* or *she.* If the antecedent is about the second person *(you),* then agreement can be achieved by using the pronoun *you.* If the antecedent is a thing, then agreement can be achieved by using the pronoun *it.*
  If <u>a person</u> wants to succeed in this game, <u>he or she</u> must know the rules.
  If <u>you</u> want to succeed in this game, <u>you</u> must know the rules.
  For <u>this game</u> to be successful, <u>it</u> needs to have specific rules.

Use the same person throughout a sentence. Throughout the discussion, maintain the point of view that begins the sentence or the text.

Inconsistent: <u>You</u> must be careful when you hike because the consequences could be deadly for <u>him or her</u>.

Consistent: <u>You</u> must be careful when you hike because the consequences could be deadly for <u>you</u>.

Pronoun Agreement with Number

If the antecedent is plural, the pronoun(s) must also be plural; if the antecedent is singular, the pronoun(s) must also be singular.
  If <u>people</u> want to succeed in this game, <u>they</u> must know the rules.
  If <u>Kayla</u> wants to succeed in this game, <u>she</u> must learn the rules.

The number agreement is most confusing when a sentence includes an indefinite pronoun or a collective noun.

1. **Indefinite pronouns are pronouns that do not indicate a definite person or thing.** Here is a list of some common indefinite pronouns:

everybody	everyone	everything	each
anybody	anyone	anything	either
somebody	someone	something	neither
nobody	no one	nothing	

Whenever these pronouns are used in a sentence, a singular pronoun (he/she or his/her) is required to refer back to them.

Incorrect:	<u>Everyone</u> must turn in <u>their</u> work.
Correct:	<u>Everyone</u> must turn in <u>his or her</u> work.
Incorrect:	<u>Each</u> of the boys brought <u>their</u> book.
Correct:	<u>Each</u> of the boys brought <u>his</u> book.
Incorrect:	Someone left <u>their</u> folder behind.
Correct:	Someone left <u>his/her</u> folder behind.

Some writers and speakers have a tendency to use the plural *their* as the reference pronoun to indefinite pronouns. This seems like an easy way to avoid the historically sexist practice of always using *his* when referring to a general person. However, since these indefinite pronouns emphasize a single body, one, or thing, the singular pronouns *he, she, his, her,* or *it* must be used.

2. **Collective nouns, such as army, team, or committee, sound plural but in reality are singular units composed of many elements.** For example, a team is a single unit made up of many players. Because it is still a "single" unit, it requires the singular pronoun *it* for reference.

The <u>army</u> deployed <u>its</u> recruits.
The <u>team</u> played <u>its</u> final game.

Pronoun Agreement with Gender

A pronoun has to agree with the masculine or feminine state of the antecedent. When a pronoun refers to a singular female noun, the pronoun must be gender-specific (*she, her*).

The <u>girl</u> turned in <u>her</u> assignment.

When a pronoun refers to a singular male noun, the pronoun must be gender-specific (*he, his*).

The <u>man</u> walked <u>his</u> dog.

Parallelism

Whenever you use a single part of speech two or more times in a sentence, each use must consistently present the part of speech in the same form. **Parallelism** in writing means that similar elements or ideas in a sentence are presented in the same form grammatically, so the reader can quickly grasp the comparison or connection being made between them. The need for parallel construction arises when your sentence contains **pairs** (two items); **lists** (three or more items); **comparisons using *than* or *as***; and **paired expressions**.

Parallelism with Pairs and Lists

You can spot pairs (two items) in sentences when you see the words *and, or.* When you use these two words, everything that comes before the *and/or* must present the same grammatical form as everything that comes after the *and/or.* The following sentences fail to achieve that balance.

I returned three books to the library <u>and</u> checking out two more.
I will drive to the library <u>or</u> rode the bus.

You need to change one of the sides to make the sentence parallel.

Correct: I returned three books to the library and checked out two more.
Correct: I will drive to the library or ride the bus.

Multiple options exist for creating parallelism in any sentence. Look at another example:

He dances <u>skillfully</u> and <u>with gracefulness.</u>

Here, the adverb *skillfully* comes before the *and* while the noun *gracefulness* comes after the *and.* The sentence will not achieve parallelism until one of these modifiers is changed.

Correct: He dances skillfully and gracefully. [adverb / adverb]
Correct: He dances with skill and grace. [noun / noun]

Parallelism must be achieved whenever pairs or lists occur in a sentence, no matter what parts of speech are involved. Here are some rules to keep in mind for specific parts of speech:

1. **Pairs and lists of verbs must be parallel in tense.**

   Incorrect: On my birthday, we sang, danced, and were eating.

   The list in this example starts with a past tense of the verb *sang;* all the verbs listed after *sang,* therefore, should also be in the past tense. *Were eating* is in the progressive past; hence, this sentence is not parallel. To correct the sentence, either change *were eating* to *ate* or change all the other verbs to past progressive.

   Correct: On my birthday, we sang, danced, and ate.
   Correct: On my birthday, we were singing, dancing, and eating.

   Note: In any list of items, be sure to use commas between each item.

2. **Pairs and lists of nouns must be parallel in number, person, and kind.**

   Incorrect: I bought coffee, some tea, and two pounds of sugar.

   The list in this example starts with a noun that has no designated measurement, followed by two nouns that do have designated measurements. This list lacks parallelism. To correct it, either add measurements to all the nouns or remove the measurements from all the nouns.

Correct: **I bought coffee, tea, and sugar.**

Correct: **I bought one pound of coffee, two pounds of tea, and five pounds of sugar.**

3. Pairs and lists of adjectives must be parallel in form.

Incorrect: **The race was dangerous, creative, and had much excitement.**

The list in this example has an adjective *(had much excitement)* which does not parallel the form of the other two adjectives in the sentence. Hence, this list is not parallel. To correct this sentence, reduce the last adjective to one word.

Correct: **The race was a dangerous, creative, and exciting.**

Parallelism with Comparisons (than or as)

To make comparisons, you must use the words *than* or *as*. When you edit for parallelism, make sure that the things being compared on either side of those words are parallel.

Incorrect: **<u>Driving</u> to school is better <u>than</u> <u>to take</u> the bus.**

The verbs on either side of *than* are not presented in the same tense. You must change one or the other to make the sentence parallel.

Correct: **<u>Driving</u> to school is better <u>than</u> <u>taking</u> the bus.**

Correct: **<u>To drive</u> to school is better <u>than</u> <u>to take</u> the bus.**

Parallelism with Paired Expressions

Paired expressions—also called correlative conjunctions—require parallel structure. These five sets of conjunctions are always paired:

Both...and

Either...or

Neither...nor

Not only...but also or but too

Rather...than

Achieve parallel construction when using paired expressing by presenting the words that follow the first conjunction in the same format as the words that follow the second conjunction.

Incorrect: **I want <u>both</u> to be wealthy <u>and</u> health.**

Correct: **I want <u>both</u> wealth <u>and</u> health.**

Correct: **I want <u>both</u> to be wealthy <u>and</u> to be healthy.**

Incorrect: **<u>Either</u> <u>we go</u> to the park <u>or</u> <u>we are going</u> to the mountains.**

Correct: **<u>Either</u> <u>we go</u> to the park <u>or</u> <u>we go</u> to the mountains.**

Correct:	Either <u>we are going</u> to the park <u>or</u> <u>we are going</u> to the mountains.
Incorrect:	He can <u>neither</u> <u>tell his</u> boss the truth <u>nor</u> <u>to quit his</u> job.
Correct:	He can <u>neither</u> <u>tell his</u> boss the truth <u>nor</u> <u>quit his</u> job.
Incorrect:	Sugar is used <u>not only</u> in cakes <u>but</u> <u>to make paste.</u>
Correct:	Sugar is used <u>not only</u> in cakes <u>but</u> also <u>in paste.</u>
Correct:	Sugar is used <u>not only</u> <u>to make cakes</u> <u>but</u> also <u>to make paste.</u>
Incorrect:	They would <u>rather</u> eat out <u>than</u> to be eating their father's cooking.
Correct:	They would <u>rather</u> <u>eat out</u> <u>than</u> <u>eat their father's cooking.</u>

Tense Consistency

You use verbs every time you write a sentence. Although the actions that take place in your paragraphs may show movement between different times, keeping to one verb tense within each sentence, paragraph, and in the overall work will avoid confusion and will help the reader follow more clearly what you are saying. To achieve this consistency, make all the verbs in the same tense as the first verb you used in the sentence.

	Simple present tense	*Present progressive tense*	*Past tense*
Incorrect:	He treats	her like a child and is laughing	at her when she did something funny.

	Simple present tense	*Simple present tense*	*Simple present tense*
Correct:	He treats	her like a child and laughs	at her when she does something funny.

OR

	Present progressive tense	*Present progressive tense*	*Present progressive tense*
	He is treating	her like a child and is laughing	at her when she is doing something funny.

III: BE CLEAR

Punctuation

Commas

Commas signal brief pauses, which help readers understand the flow of thought or action in a sentence. Beginning writers may use either too few or too many commas, so their sentences are unclear or difficult to read. Commas are used for two purposes: to separate and to enclose.

Commas Used to Separate

Commas create a small but necessary amount of separation between items on a list and phrases that introduce or lead up to an independent clause. They are also used to create a necessary pause between two independent clauses, allowing readers time to separate and compare them in their minds.

1. **Commas and items in a list.**

   Use commas to separate items in a list (three or more items). This includes the last item in the series which usually has either the word *and*, or the word *or* before it.

   Series of nouns: **I bought coffee, tea, flour, and sugar.**

   Series of verbs: **At the meeting, I ate, drank, and mingled with my supervisors.**

2. **Commas and introductory expressions.**

   An introductory expression is a phrase composed of one word (*finally, oh, however*) or a group of words (*by the end of the day* or *as we all know*). It comes at the beginning of a sentence, and it never contains the subject and verb that create the basic meaning of the sentence. In other words, if you were to take an introductory expression out of the sentence, the remaining part of the sentence would make sense on its own. Use a comma after an introductory expression to let your readers know which part of the sentence is the main one or the one that makes sense on its own.

   <u>Nonetheless</u>, I must take this in to the inspector.

   <u>By the way</u>, I spoke to Tim today.

   <u>According to Mr. Smith</u>, the case is about to be closed.

3. **Commas and conjunctions.**

   There are three types of conjunctions, and with each type, you must use commas in different locations to separate the clauses.

   - **Coordinating conjunctions** join two independent clauses and require a comma before the conjunction.

     John finished his essay, <u>but</u> Brian is still working on his.

   - **Adverbial conjunctions** join two or more independent clauses and require a semicolon before the conjunction and a comma after the conjunction.

     Kim went to the party; <u>however</u>, she did not stay long.

   - **Subordinating conjunctions** join an independent clause with a dependent clause and require a comma only if the conjunction is at the beginning of the sentence.

     <u>When</u> I got home, I saw the mess the robbers had left behind.
     [Comma needed]

     I saw the mess the robbers had left behind <u>when</u> I got home.
     [No comma needed]

Commas to Enclose

Words or phrases that are not essential to the basic understanding of a sentence must be enclosed, or surrounded, by commas.

1. **Commas and interrupters.** An interrupter is a word or a group of words that appears in the middle of the sentence but which, like an introductory expression, does not contain the subject or verb necessary to the basic meaning of the sentence. Interrupters might be called "scoopables" as a way of thinking about their purpose in a sentence—the words can be scooped out of the sentence without changing the basic meaning of the sentence. Interrupters may separate the subject and the verb and may break the sentence's flow—sometimes for dramatic effect—but they do not add to or subtract from the basic grammatical meaning.

   Use commas before and after an interrupter to enclose or set off the "scoopable" from the subject and verb of the sentence.

   I must take this, <u>nonetheless</u>, and show it to the inspector.

   I spoke to Tim, <u>by the way</u>, and he agreed to come.

   The criminal case, <u>according to Mr. Smith</u>, is about to be closed.

2. **Commas and direct address.** When the speaker in a sentence talks to another person and names that person, the process is called direct address because the speaker is directly addressing his or her audience. Put commas around the name that appears in the sentence.

   <u>John</u>, may I stop by your office today?

   I think, <u>Jim</u>, you are mistaken about the situation.

   Your grades are excellent, <u>Manny</u>!

   Note: If the name is the subject in the sentence, do not separate the subject from the verb with a comma unless there is an interrupter.

   Incorrect: **John, is my friend.**
   Correct: **John is my friend.**

   Here, the sentence is talking *about* John, not to John, so the name is the subject in the sentence, and the subject cannot be separated from the verb with a comma.

3. **Commas with dates and addresses.**

   a. Use a comma to separate the month and day from the year.
      I was born on November 15, 2001.

      November 15 is one day out of 365 days of the calendar year 2001. That is, it is one day inside of that year, so a comma is needed to separate the day from the year and to indicate that the specific day falls inside that specific year.

Also, if you include the name of a day in your date, separate it from the other elements with a comma.

I was elected on Tuesday, November 4, 2008.

Note: Do not use a comma if just the month and year are given.

I was elected in November 2008.

   b. Use a comma to separate elements of an address included in a sentence or to separate the city from the state.

I live on 100 W. Pine Street, Covina, California 91520.

I lived in Dallas, Texas.

Note: No comma is needed between the state and zip code.

Apostrophes

The **apostrophe** is a mark that looks exactly like a comma but is raised and placed between letters in a word rather than between whole words. Apostrophes allow you to write more efficiently, with fewer words, in two specific situations:

1. **To show possession.** An apostrophe allows you to take a wordy sentence like *The jacket belongs to Jim,* and shorten into the phrase *Jim's jacket.* Whenever you need to show that something or someone owns or possesses something or someone else, <u>always</u> use an apostrophe and <u>sometimes</u> add an *–s*. Grammar has established clear rules for how to tell when you need to add the *–s*:

   a. To show ownership with singular nouns, use the apostrophe and *–s*.

Jim's jacket	**Girl's coat**	**Jess's hat**
Everybody's turn	**Anyone's question**	

   b. To show possession or ownership with plural nouns that do not end in *–s* or *–es*, use an apostrophe and add an *–s*.

Men's cologne	**People's concern**	**Children's clothing**

   c. To show possession with plural nouns ending with *–s*, use only an apostrophe.

Girls' coats	**Teams' coaches**

   d. When two nouns are involved, apostrophes must show whether the subjects have joint or individual ownership.

   My brother and sister's car (they share the same car)

   My brother's and sister's cars (they each own a separate car)

e. To show possession with personal pronouns, do not use an apostrophe at all.

Yours is my favorite painting in the gallery.

Whose wallet is this?

2. **To show contractions.** Contractions are handy for shortening or contracting two words into one. Use an apostrophe to indicate the position of the missing letter or letters. The following verbs are often used in a contracted form:

Verbs with *not*	can not = can't are not = aren't	was not = wasn't do not = don't
Pronouns with *will*	I will = I'll you will = you'll	she will = she'll they will = they'll
Pronouns and nouns with the verb *to be*	it is = it's I am = I'm	who is = who's Mark is = Mark's
Pronouns with *would*	I would = I'd he would = he'd	we would = we'd they would = they'd

Note: One special contraction changes letters as well as drops them: *Will not* becomes *won't* in the contracted form.

3. **To form the plurals of letters and figures.**

Cross your *t*'s.   Her *p*'s and *q*'s all look the same.

Spelling

To become a better speller, always proofread your writing and follow five important strategies.

Proofreading

Proofreading is checking a piece of writing for accuracy and correctness. Its purpose is to catch any careless mistakes that might distract or confuse readers. Proofreading is best done after all substantial changes, improvements, and additions have been made to the paper. Try the following techniques:

- Print out your writing and proofread on hard copy.
- Read your paper aloud.
- Ask someone else to read your paper aloud, and listen carefully as he or she reads.
- Run your writing through a spell-check program.
- Read your text backward. Turn to the last line of your paper, hold a ruler or pencil over the line just above, and move it up as you read from the bottom up, checking one word at a time.

Spelling Strategies

1. **Create spelling lists.** Create a list of words you have trouble with and update the list as you encounter new words. Check to see whether a word that you find troublesome shares a root, prefix, or suffix with a word you already know; the connection helps you learn the meaning, as well as the spelling, of the new word.

2. **Learn the ei/ie rule.** Write *i* before *e* except after *c* (or when it sounds like *a* as in neighbor or weigh).

i **before** *e*:	chief	piece	brief	yield	priest
after *c*:	ceiling	receive	receipt	perceive	deceive
sounds like *a*:	eight	freight	vein	their	neighbor

Note: Four exceptions exist to this rule: *leisure, seizure, foreign,* and *height* all have *ei* spellings, though none of the four come after *c* or sound like *a*.

3. **Know commonly misspelled words.** Many words are misspelled because of their unusual letter combinations or incorrect pronunciation. Study this list to strengthen your ability to spot and avoid misspellings:

Incorrect	Correct
sincerly	sincerely
fourty	forty
libary	library
payed	paid
judgement	judgment
coperate	cooperate
goverment	government
seperate	separate
necesary	necessary
privaledge	privilege

4. **Know commonly confused words.** Words that sound alike or look alike can cause frequent spelling errors. Here's a list of confusing pairs of words.

Accept: to receive (verb)   I accept your decision.
Except: other than (preposition)   I greeted everyone except you.

Advice: guidance (noun)   I like your advice.
Advise: to give guidance (verb)   She advised me to drop the class.

Affect: to influence (verb)
Effect: result (noun)

The pollution affects our lungs.
Pollution has a strong effect on our lungs.

All ready: all (pronoun) are ready (adverb)
Already: before (adverb)

The passengers were all ready to board the ship.
I did this assignment already.

Brake: to stop (verb)
Break: to come apart (verb)

The train brakes at railroad signs.
That vase breaks easily.

Capital: city or money (noun)

Sacramento is the capital of California.
He raised capital for his business venture.

Capitol: a building (noun)

Washington has a capitol building.

Clothes: apparel (noun)
Cloths: fabric (plural noun)

I wear my clothes.
My clothes are made from cloths.

Conscience: moral guide (noun)
Conscious: awake or aware (adverb)

Lies are against my conscience.
The accident victim was not conscious.

Desert: dry land (noun)
Dessert: sweet food (noun)

The desert climate is hot.
Apple pie is a great dessert.

Heard: past tense of *to hear* (verb)
Herd: a group of animals (noun)

I heard a rumor about the war.
The herd of cows is let out.

Knew: past tense of *to know* (verb)
New: recent, not old (adjective)

I knew a sweet man.
My new boots squeak.

Loose: not too tight (adjective)
Lose: not to win (verb)

My pants are loose on my waist.
I always lose at Scrabble.

Personal: private (adjective)
Personnel: employees (plural noun)

This is a personal matter.
The personnel at the company are frustrated.

Principal: leader (noun)
Principle: rule or concept (noun)

She is the principal of our school.
America is based on the principle of democracy.

Quite: entirely or very (adverb)   The dress is quite lovely.
Quiet: silent (adjective)   He is a quiet person.
Quit: to stop (verb)   I quit my job.

Then: next in time (adverb)   We danced then ate.
Than: to compare (conjunction)   He is shorter than Doris.

Thought: past tense of *to think* (verb)   I thought of him always.
Though: form of *although* (conjunction)   Though he is gone, I still love him.

Weather: climate (noun)   The weather is cold.
Whether: either or in case (conjunction)   We should know whether it will rain tonight.

5. **Know the word endings.** Sometimes, the spelling error occurs in how we spell the end of a word. This occurs most commonly when we are changing a word from the singular to the plural form. Here are a few guidelines to keep in mind:

   - For words ending in *s, ss, x, z, sh,* or *ch* add an *–es.*
     boxes   churches   mistresses   fizzes   dishes

   - For words ending in *f* or *fe,* change the *f* to *y* and add *–es.*
     shelf   shelves   wife   wives

   - For words ending in *o* preceded by a vowel (*a,e,i,o,u*) add *–s.* For words ending in *o* preceded by a consonant, add *–es.*
     with vowels: zoo   zoos   rodeo   rodeos
     with consonant: hero   heroes   tomato   tomatoes

   - For words ending in *y,* change the *y* to *i* and add *–es.*
     city   cities   lily   lilies   candy   candies

   - For some words, no ending is required to show the plural form.
     fish   sheep   series   deer

   - For some words, we change the whole word, not just the ending.
     child   children   man   men   tooth   teeth

   - For Greek and Latin nouns, there are special spellings to show plural form.
     datum   data   thesis   theses   criterion
     syllabus   syllabi   analysis   analyses   criteria

Common Sentence Errors

Fragments

A complete sentence must contain both a subject and a verb. A **fragment** is an incomplete sentence that does not make sense and cannot stand on its own. A fragment has one of the following five problems.

1. **The sentence is missing a subject.**
   Can't be my friend. (fragment)
   <u>Tom</u> cannot be my friend. (complete sentence)

   Remember that a subject can be a person, place, thing, or idea.

   Doesn't have to lead to bitter fights. (fragment)
   <u>Expressing a political opinion</u> doesn't have to lead to bitter fights. (complete sentence)

   A subject can also be a pronoun.

   <u>This</u> does not have to lead to bitter fights. (complete sentence)

2. **The sentence is missing a verb.**
   The girl in the red hood. (fragment)
   The girl with the red hood <u>walked</u> toward me. (complete sentence)

   Remember that a verb can be a state of being as well as an action.

   Unselfish love toward another human being. (fragment)
   Unselfish love toward another human being <u>is rare</u>. (complete sentence)

3. **The sentence is missing both a subject and a verb.**
   At the end of the day. (fragment)
   On the soccer field. (fragment)
   To play the piano. (fragment)

   To fix the fragment, add an independent clause (which by definition contains both a subject and a verb) to the phrase.

   At the end of the day, <u>Gina watches the sun set</u>. (complete sentence)
   <u>The players cheered</u> on the soccer field. (complete sentence)
   <u>I am longing</u> to play the piano. (complete sentence)

4. **The sentence is missing a helping verb.** The sentence has an *–ing* verb with no helping verb (*is, are, was, were, has, have, had*...).
   Barry running to the door. (fragment)

   To fix the fragment, add a helping verb.

   Barry <u>kept</u> running to the door. (complete sentence)

5. **The sentence is a dependent clause which cannot stand alone.** Even though it contains both a subject and a verb, a dependent clause does not express a complete thought.

> **When the band started to play.** (fragment)
> **While she talked on the phone.** (fragment)
> **That Jerry described.** (fragment)

To fix the fragment, add an independent clause.

> **When the band started to play, <u>people got up to dance</u>.** (complete sentence)
> **<u>Jerry interrupted her</u> while she talked on the phone.** (complete sentence)
> **<u>She couldn't understand the directions</u> that Jerry described.** (complete sentence)

Run-ons

Run-ons, also called run-together sentences, are sentence errors made up of two side-by-side independent clauses that have no punctuation between them. The lack of punctuation makes it difficult for a reader to follow the movement from one complete thought to the other.

> **We did not hear about the party until Friday we had to quickly change our plans.**

Placing a conjunction between the two clauses helps but is still difficult to follow.

> **We did not hear about the party until Friday <u>so</u> we had to quickly change our plans.**

Punctuation must also be added to create a big enough pause for the reader's brain to correctly understand the sentence:

> **We did not hear about the party till Friday<u>, so</u> we had to quickly change our plans.**

To fix run-ons, use one of the following solutions:

1. **Add a period between the two independent clauses.**
   > **We didn't hear about the party until Friday<u>.</u> We had to change our plans.**
2. **Add a semicolon between the two independent clauses.**
   > **We had to change our plans<u>;</u> we didn't hear about the party until Friday.**
3. **Add a conjunction and punctuate correctly.**
   a. , + coordinating conjunction
   > **We didn't hear about the party until Friday<u>, so</u> we had to change our plans.**

b. ; + adverbial conjunction + ,

> We didn't hear of the party until Friday; <u>therefore,</u> we changed our plans.

c. subordinating conjunction with or without comma

> <u>When</u> we heard about the party, we changed our plans.
> We changed our plans <u>when</u> we heard about the party.

Comma Splices

Comma splices are sentence errors made up of two side-by-side independent clauses with only a comma separating them. The comma interrupts the reader's movement from one complete thought to the other.

> The storm hit sooner than expected, the race was cancelled.

Placing a conjunction between the two clauses helps, but it is still difficult to follow if the conjunction is not punctuated correctly.

> The storm hit sooner than expected <u>yet,</u> the race was cancelled.

The conjunction must be added in the right place relative to the comma, so a big enough pause is created for the reader's brain to correctly understand the sentence.

> The storm hit sooner than expected<u>, yet</u> the race was cancelled.

To fix comma splices, use one of the following solutions:

1. **Add a period between the two independent clauses.**

> The storm hit sooner than expected<u>.</u> The race was cancelled.

2. **Add a semicolon between the two independent clauses.**

> The storm hit sooner than expected<u>;</u> the race was cancelled.

3. **Add a conjunction and punctuate correctly.**

   a. , + coordinating conjunction

   > The storm hit sooner than expected<u>, and</u> the race was cancelled.

   b. ; + adverbial conjunction + ,

   > The storm hit sooner than expected; <u>consequently,</u> the race was cancelled.

   c. subordinating conjunction with or without comma

   > <u>Since</u> the storm hit sooner than expected, the race was cancelled.
   > The storm hit sooner than expected <u>before</u> the race was cancelled.

APPENDIX B: Commonly Used Transitions

GENERAL

certainly	indeed	no doubt
of course	to be sure	also
besides	in fact	moreover
furthermore	next	then
in addition		

EXAMPLE

one example	another example	most important example
for example	in other words	namely
specifically	to illustrate	for instance

EFFECT

first effect	second effect	most important effect
consequently	as a result	thus
therefore		

CAUSE

first reason	second reason	most important reason
accordingly	one reason	another reason
because	then	so

COMPARISON

as well	equally	likewise
similarly		

CONTRAST

however	in contrast	instead
nevertheless	on the contrary	as opposed to
on the other hand		

EMPHASIS/IMPORTANCE

clearly	above all	in fact
in particular	indeed	least of all
most of all	undoubtedly	especially
most importantly		

SPACE

above	at the back	behind
below	beside	closer in
farther out	in front	in the middle
inside	nearby	on the bottom
on the left/right	on top	outside
under		

TIME

after that	at that time	at the moment
currently	earlier	eventually
first	gradually	immediately
in the future	in the past	later
meanwhile	now	one day
presently	so far	suddenly
then	these days	nowadays

CONCLUSION

generally	in other words	in short
on the whole	therefore	thus

Index